# CRITIQUE OF THE GOTHA PROGRAMME

# CRITIQUE OF THE

# GOTHA PROGRAMME

By
**KARL MARX**

*With Appendices by
Marx, Engels and Lenin*

A REVISED TRANSLATION

**NEW YORK**
**INTERNATIONAL PUBLISHERS**

Edited *by* C. P. Dutt

COPYRIGHT, 1938

INTERNATIONAL PUBLISHERS CO., INC.

———

PRINTED IN THE U. S. A.

*Composed and Printed by Union Labor*

# PUBLISHERS' NOTE

The present edition of Marx's "Notes on the Programme of the German Workers' Party" (*Critique of the Gotha Programme*) includes a number of chapters from Lenin's *The State and Revolution* which deal directly with the *Critique,* and extracts from Lenin's notebook *Marxism on the State.* The text of the draft of the so-called Gotha Programme is also given. This programme was put before the Congress held in Gotha (May 22-27, 1875), which united the Social-Democratic Workers' Party of Germany (the so-called Eisenachers) led by W. Liebknecht and Bebel, and the General Association of German Workers, which had been founded by Lassalle.

Marx sent his criticism of the Gotha Programme to W. Bracke on May 5, 1875, requesting that it be passed on to the other leaders of the Eisenach party (see Marx's letter to Bracke in this volume). Marx's original manuscript of the *Critique* has not been preserved. Only a copy in an unknown handwriting was found among Engels' papers. This copy was the one that was published in 1891 by Engels. The translation for the present edition has been made from this text.

The present edition is a revised translation of an earlier edition issued by International Publishers in 1933, and is based upon the Russian edition of the Marx-Engels-Lenin Institute.

The translation of the chapters from Lenin's *The State and Revolution* and of the extracts from *Marxism on the State* has been made from the Russian text published by the Marx-Engels-Lenin Institute.

# CONTENTS

# CRITIQUE OF THE GOTHA PROGRAMME

# CRITIQUE OF THE GOTHA PROGRAMME

## Marginal Notes to the Programme of the German Workers' Party

## I.

1. "Labour is the source of all wealth and all culture *and since* useful labour is only possible in society and through society, the proceeds of labour belong undiminished with equal right to all members of society."

*First Part of the Paragraph:* "Labour is the source of all wealth and all culture."

Labour is *not the source* of all wealth. *Nature* is just as much the source of use values (and it is surely of such that material wealth consists!) as is labour, which itself is only the manifestation of a natural force, human labour power.[1] That phrase is to be found in all children's primers and is correct in so far as it is *implied* that labour proceeds with the appropriate subjects and instruments. But a socialist programme cannot allow such bourgeois phrases to cause the *conditions* to be ignored that alone give them meaning. And in so far as man from the beginning behaves towards nature, the primary source of all instruments and subjects of labour, as her owner, treats her as belonging to him, his labour becomes the source of use values, therefore also of wealth. The bourgeois have very good grounds for fancifully ascribing *supernatural creative power* to labour, since it follows precisely from the fact that labour depends on nature, that the man who possesses no other property than his labour power must, in all conditions of society and culture, be the slave of other men who have made themselves the owners of the material conditions of labour. He can only work with their permission, and hence only live with their permission.[2]

3

Let us now leave the sentence as it stands, or rather limps. What would one have expected as conclusion? Obviously this:

"Since labour is the source of all wealth, in society also no one can appropriate wealth except as the product of labour. Therefore, if he himself does not work, he lives by the labour of others and also acquires his culture at the expense of the labour of others."

Instead of this, by means of the words *"and since"* a second proposition is added in order to draw a conclusion from this and not from the first one.

*Second Part of the Paragraph:* "Useful labour is only possible in society and through society."

According to the first proposition, labour was the source of all wealth and all culture, therefore also no society is possible without labour. Now we learn, conversely, that no "useful" labour is possible without society.

One could just as well have said that only in society can useless and even generally harmful labour become a branch of gainful occupation, that only in society can one live by being idle, etc., etc.; —in short one could just as well have copied the whole of Rousseau.[3]

And what is "useful" labour? Surely only labour which produces the intended useful effect. A savage—and man was a savage after he had ceased to be an ape—who has killed an animal with a stone, who collects fruits, etc., performs "useful" labour.

*Thirdly: The Conclusion:* "And since useful labour is only possible in society and through society—the proceeds of labour belong undiminished with equal right to all members of society."

A fine conclusion! If useful labour is only possible in society and through society, the proceeds of labour belong to society—and only so much therefrom accrues to the individual worker as is not required to maintain the "condition" of labour, society.

In fact, also, this proposition has at all times been made use of by the champions of the *prevailing state of society*. First come the claims of the government and everything connected with it, since it is the social organ for the maintenance of the social order; then come the claims of the various kinds of private property, for the various kinds of private property are the foundations of society, etc. One sees that such hollow phrases can be twisted and turned as desired.

The first and second parts of the paragraph have some intelligible connection only in the following wording:

"Labour only becomes the source of wealth and culture as social labour," or, what is the same thing, "in and through society."

This proposition is incontestably correct, for although isolated labour (its material conditions presupposed) can also create use values, it can create neither wealth nor culture.

But equally incontestable is this other proposition:

"In proportion as labour develops socially, and becomes thereby a source of wealth and culture, poverty and neglect develop among the workers, and wealth and culture among the non-workers."

This is the law of all history hitherto. What, therefore, had to be done here, instead of making general phrases about "labour" and "society," was to prove concretely how in present capitalist society the material, etc., conditions have at last been created which will enable and compel the workers to lift this social curse.

In fact, however, the whole paragraph, incorrect in style and content, is only there in order to inscribe the Lassallean [4] catch-word of the "undiminished proceeds of labour" as a slogan at the top of the party banner. I shall return to the "proceeds of labour," "equal right," etc., later on, since the same thing recurs in a somewhat different form.

2. "In present-day society, the instruments of labour are the monopoly of the capitalist class; the resulting dependence of the working class is the cause of misery and servitude in all its forms."

This sentence, borrowed from the Statutes of the International,[5] is incorrect in this "improved" edition.

In present-day society the instruments of labour are the monopoly of the landowners (the monopoly of property in land is even the basis of the monopoly of capital) *and* the capitalists. In the passage in question, the Statutes of the International do not mention by name either the one or the other class of monopolists. They speak of the *"monopoly of the means of labour, that is the sources of life."* The addition, *"sources of life"* makes it sufficiently clear that land is included in the instruments of labour.

The correction was introduced because Lassalle, for reasons now generally known, attacked *only* the capitalist class and not the land-owners.[6] In England, the capitalist is usually not even the owner of the land on which his factory stands.

 3. "The emancipation of labour demands the promotion of the instruments of labour to the common property of society, and the co-operative regulation of the total labour with equitable distribution of the proceeds of labour."

"Promotion of the instruments of labour to the common property" ought obviously to read, their "conversion into the common property," but this only in passing.

What are the "proceeds of labour"? The product of labour or its value? And in the latter case, is it the total value of the product or only that part of the value which labour has newly added to the value of the means of production consumed?[7]

The "proceeds of labour" is a loose notion which Lassalle has put in the place of definite economic conceptions.

What is "equitable distribution"?

Do not the bourgeois assert that the present-day distribution is "equitable"? And is it not, in fact, the only "equitable" distribution on the basis of the present-day mode of production? Are economic relations regulated by legal conceptions or do not, on the contrary, legal relations arise from economic ones? Have not also the socialist sectarians[8] the most varied notions about "equitable" distribution?

To understand what idea is meant in this connection by the phrase "equitable distribution," we must take the first paragraph and this one together. The latter implies a society wherein "the instruments of labour are common property, and the total labour is co-operatively regulated," and from the first paragraph we learn that "the proceeds of labour belong undiminished with equal right to all members of society."

"To all members of society"? To those who do not work as well? What remains then of the "undiminished proceeds of labour"? Only to those members of society who work? What remains then of the "equal right" of all members of society?

But "all members of society" and "equal right" are obviously mere phrases. The kernel consists in this, that in this communist society every worker must receive the "undiminished" Lassallean "proceeds of labour."

Let us take first of all the words "proceeds of labour" in the sense of the product of labour, then the co-operative proceeds of labour are the *total social product.*

From this is then to be deducted:

*First,* cover for replacement of the means of production used up.

*Secondly,* additional portion for expansion of production.

*Thirdly,* reserve or insurance fund to provide against mis-adventures, disturbances through natural events, etc.

These deductions from the "undiminished proceeds of labour" are an economic necessity and their magnitude is to be determined by available means and forces, and partly by calculation of probabilities, but they are in no way calculable by equity.

There remains the other part of the total product, destined to serve as means of consumption.

Before this is divided among the individuals, there has to be deducted from it:

*First, the general costs of administration not belonging to production.*

This part will, from the outset, be very considerably restricted in comparison with present-day society and it diminishes in proportion as the new society develops.

*Secondly, that which is destined for the communal satisfaction of needs, such as schools, health services, etc.*

From the outset this part is considerably increased in comparison with present-day society and it increases in proportion as the new society develops.

*Thirdly, funds for those unable to work, etc.,* in short, what is included under so-called official poor relief today.

Only now do we come to the "distribution" which the programme, under Lassallean influence, alone has in view in its narrow fashion, namely that part of the means of consumption which is divided among the individual producers of the co-operative society.[9]

The "undiminished proceeds of labour" have already quietly become converted into the "diminished" proceeds, although what the producer is deprived of in his capacity as a private individual benefits him directly or indirectly in his capacity as a member of society.

Just as the phrase "undiminished proceeds of labour" has disappeared, so now does the phrase "proceeds of labour" disappear altogether.[10]

Within the co-operative society based on common ownership of the means of production, the producers do not exchange their products; just as little does the labour employed on the products appear here *as the value* of these products, as a material quality possessed by them, since now, in contrast to capitalist society, individual labour no longer exists in an indirect fashion but directly as a component part of the total labour. The phrase "proceeds of labour," objectionable even today on account of its ambiguity, thus loses all meaning.

What we have to deal with here is a communist society, not as it has *developed* on its own foundations, but, on the contrary, as it *emerges* from capitalist society; which is thus in every respect, economically, morally and intellectually, still stamped with the birthmarks of the old society from whose womb it emerges. Accordingly the individual producer receives back from society—after the deductions have been made—exactly what he gives to it. What he has given to it is his individual amount of labour. For example, the social working day consists of the sum of the individual labour hours; the individual labour time of the individual producer is the part of the social labour day contributed by him, his share in it. He receives a certificate from society that he has furnished such and such an amount of labour (after deducting his labour for the common fund), and with this certificate he draws from the social stock of means of consumption as much as the same amount of labour costs. The same amount of labour which he has given to society in one form, he receives back in another.

Here obviously the same principle prevails as that which regulates the exchange of commodities, as far as this is exchange of equal values. Content and form are changed, because under the altered circumstances no one can give anything except his labour, and because, on the other hand, nothing can pass into the ownership of individuals except individual means of consumption. But, as far as the distribution of the latter among the individual producers is concerned, the same principle prevails as in the exchange of commodity-equivalents, so much labour in one form is exchanged for an equal amount of labour in another form.

Hence, *equal right* here is still in principle—*bourgeois right*, although principle and practice are no longer in conflict, while the exchange of equivalents in commodity exchange only exists on the *average* and not in the individual case.

In spite of this advance, this *equal right* is still stigmatised by a bourgeois limitation. The right of the producers is *proportional* to the labour they supply; the equality consists in the fact that measurement is made with an *equal standard*, labour.

But one man is superior to another physically or mentally and so supplies more labour in the same time, or can labour for a longer time; and labour, to serve as a measure, must be defined by its duration or intensity, otherwise it ceases to be a standard of measurement. This *equal* right is an unequal right for unequal labour. It recognises no class differences, because everyone is only a worker like everyone else; but it tacitly recognises unequal individual endowment and thus productive capacity as natural privileges. *It is therefore a right of inequality in its content, like every right.* Right by its very nature can only consist in the application of an equal standard; but unequal individuals (and they would not be different individuals if they were not unequal) are only measurable by an equal standard in so far as they are brought under an equal point of view, are taken from one *definite* side only, *e.g.*, in the present case are regarded *only as workers*, and nothing more seen in them, everything else being ignored. Further, one worker is married, another not; one has more children than another and so on and so forth. Thus with an equal output, and hence an equal share in the social consumption fund, one will in fact receive more than another, one will be richer than another, and so on. To avoid all these defects, right, instead of being equal, would have to be unequal.[11]

But these defects are inevitable in the first phase of communist society as it is when it has just emerged after prolonged birth pangs from capitalist society. Right can never be higher than the economic structure of society and the cultural development thereby determined.[12]

In a higher phase of communist society, after the enslaving subordination of individuals under division of labour, and therewith also the antithesis between mental and physical labour, has vanished; after labour, from a mere means of life, has itself become the prime necessity of life; after the productive forces have also increased with the all-round development of the individual, and all the springs of co-operative wealth flow more abundantly—only then can the narrow horizon of bourgeois right be fully left behind and society inscribe on its banners: from each according to his ability, to each according to his needs![13]

I have dealt more at length with the "undiminished proceeds of labour" on the one hand, and with "equal right" and "equitable distribution" on the other, in order to show what a crime it is to attempt, on the one hand, to force on our party again, as dogmas, ideas which in a certain period had some meaning but have now become obsolete rubbishy phrases, while on the other, perverting the realistic outlook, which has cost so much effort to instill into the party, but which has now taken root in it, by means of ideological nonsense about "right" and other trash common among the democrats and French Socialists.

Quite apart from the analysis so far given, it was in general incorrect to make a fuss about so-called *"distribution"* and put the principal stress on it.

The distribution of the means of consumption at any time is only a consequence of the distribution of the conditions of production themselves. The latter distribution, however, is a feature of the mode of production itself. The capitalist mode of production, for example, rests on the fact that the material conditions of production are in the hands of non-workers in the form of property in capital and land, while the masses are only owners of the personal condition of production, *viz.*, labour power. Once the elements of production are so distributed, then the present-day distribution of the means of consumption results automatically. If the material conditions of production are the co-operative property of the workers themselves, then this likewise results in a different distribution of the means of consumption from the present one. Vulgar socialism (and from it in turn a section of democracy) has taken over from the bourgeois economists the consideration and treatment of distribution as independent of the mode of production and hence the presentation of socialism as turning principally on distribution.[14] After the real position has long been made clear, why go back again?

4. "The emancipation of labour must be the work of the working class, in contrast to which all other classes are *only one reactionary mass.*"

The first strophe is taken from the introductory words of the Statutes of the International, but "improved." There it is said: "The emancipation of the working class must be the act of the workers themselves."[15] Here, on the contrary, the "working class" has to emancipate—what? "Labour." Let him who can understand.

In compensation, the antistrophe[16] on the other hand is a Lassallean quotation of the first water: "in contrast to which (the working class) all other classes *form only one reactionary mass.*"[17]

In *The Communist Manifesto* it is said: "Of all the classes that stand face to face with the bourgeoisie today, the proletariat alone is a *really revolutionary class*. The other classes decay and finally disappear in the face of modern industry, the proletariat is its special and essential product."[18]

The bourgeoisie is here conceived as a revolutionary class—as the bearer of large-scale industry—in contrast to the feudal lords and middle estates, who desire to maintain all social positions that are the creation of obsolete modes of production. Thus they do not form *together* with the *bourgeoisie* only one reactionary mass.

On the other hand, the proletariat is revolutionary in contrast to the bourgeoisie because, having itself grown up on the basis of large-scale industry, it strives to strip off from production the capitalist character that the bourgeoisie seeks to perpetuate. But the *Manifesto* adds that the "middle class ... if by chance they are revolutionary, they are so only in view of their impending transfer into the proletariat." [19]

From this point of view, therefore, it is again nonsense to say that they, together with the bourgeoisie, and with the feudal lords into the bargain, "form only one reactionary mass" in relation to the working class.

Did we proclaim to the artisans, small industrialists, etc., and *peasants* during the last elections: [20] In contrast to us you, with the bourgeois and feudal lords, form only one reactionary mass?

Lassalle knew *The Communist Manifesto* by heart, as his faithful followers know the gospels written by him. If, therefore, he has falsified it so grossly, this has occurred only to put a good colour on his alliance with absolutist and feudal opponents against the bourgeoisie.[21]

In the above paragraph, moreover, his oracular saying is dragged in by force without any connection with the botched quotation from the Statutes of the International. Thus it is here simply an impertinence and indeed not at all displeasing to Herr Bismarck, one of those cheap pieces of insolence in which the Marat [22] of Berlin deals.

5. "The working class strives for its emancipation first of all *within the framework of the present-day national state,* conscious that the necessary result of its efforts, which are common to the workers of all civilised countries, will be the international brotherhood of peoples."

Lassalle, in opposition to *The Communist Manifesto* and to all earlier socialism, conceived the workers' movement from the narrowest national standpoint. He is being followed in this—and that after the work of the International! [23]

It is altogether self-evident that, to be able to fight at all, the working class must organise itself at home *as a class* and that its own country is the immediate arena of its struggle. So far its class struggle is national, not in content, but, as *The Communist Manifesto* says, "in form."[24] But the "framework of the present-day national state," *e.g.*, the German empire, is itself in its turn economically "within the framework" of the world market, politically "within the framework" of the system of states. Every businessman knows that German trade is at the same time foreign trade, and the greatness of Herr Bismarck consists, to be sure, precisely in a kind of *international* policy.[25]

And to what does the German Workers' Party reduce its internationalism? To the consciousness that the result of its efforts will be *"the international brotherhood of peoples"*—a phrase borrowed from the bourgeois League of Peace and Freedom,[26] which is intended to pass as equivalent to the international brotherhood of the working classes in the joint struggle against the ruling classes and their governments. Not a word, therefore, *about the international functions* of the German working class! And it is in this way it is to challenge its own bourgeoisie, which is already linked up in brotherhood against it with the bourgeois of all other countries, and Herr Bismarck's international policy of conspiracy![27]

In fact the international consciousness expressed in the programme stands *even infinitely below* that of the Free Trade Party. The latter also asserts that the result of its efforts will be "the international brotherhood of peoples." But it also *does* something to make trade international and by no means contents itself with the consciousness —that all peoples are carrying on trade at home.

The international activity of the working classes does not in any way depend on the existence of the International Workingmen's Association. This was only the first attempt to create a central organ for that activity; an attempt which was of lasting success on account of the impulse which it gave but which was no longer realisable in its *first historical form* after the fall of the Paris Commune.

Bismarck's *Norddeutsche*[28] was absolutely correct when it announced for the satisfaction of its master that the German Workers' Party had repudiated internationalism in the new programme.[29]

## II.

"Starting from these basic principles, the German Workers' Party strives by all legal means for the *free state—and—*socialist society; the abolition of the wage system *together with* the *iron law of wages*—and—exploitation in every form; the removal of all social and political inequality."

I shall return to the "free" state later.

Thus, in future, the German Workers' Party has got to believe in Lassalle's "iron law of wages!" [30] That this shall not be lost, the nonsense is perpetrated of speaking of the "abolition of the wage system" (it should read: system of wage labour) *together with* the "iron law of wages." If I abolish wage labour, then naturally I abolish its laws also, whether they are of "iron" or sponge. But Lassalle's attack on wage labour turns almost solely on this so-called law. In order, therefore, to prove that Lassalle's sect has conquered, the "wage system" must be abolished "*together* with the iron law of wages" and not without it.

It is well known that nothing of the "iron law of wages" belongs to Lassalle except the word "iron" borrowed from Goethe's "great, eternal, iron laws." The word *iron* is a label by which the true believers recognise one another. But if I take the law with Lassalle's stamp on it and consequently in his sense then I must also take it with his basis for it. And what is that? As Lange [31] already showed, shortly after Lassalle's death, it is the Malthusian [32] theory of population (preached by Lange himself). But if this theory is correct, then again I can *not* abolish the law even if I abolish wage labour a hundred times over, because the law then governs not only the system of wage labour but *every* social system. Basing themselves directly on this, the economists have proved for fifty years and more that socialism cannot abolish poverty, *which has its basis in nature,* but can only *generalise* it, distribute it simultaneously over the whole surface of society!

But all this is not the main thing. Quite *apart* from this *false*

Lassallean formulation of the law, the truly infuriating retrograde step consists in the following:

Since Lassalle's death [33] the scientific understanding has made progress in *our* party that wages are not what they *appear* to be, namely, the *value*, or *price*, *of labour*, but only a masked form for the *value*, or *price*, *of labour power*. Thereby the whole bourgeois conception of wages hitherto, as well as all the criticism hitherto directed against this conception, was thrown overboard once for all and it was made clear that the wage worker has permission to work for his own life, *i.e.*, *to live*, only in so far as he works for a certain time gratis for the capitalist (and hence also for the latter's fellow consumers of surplus value); that the whole capitalist system of production turns on the prolongation of this gratis labour by extending the working day or by developing the productivity, *i.e.*, the greater intensity of labour power, etc., that, consequently, the system of wage labour is a system of slavery, and indeed a slavery which becomes more severe in proportion as the social productive forces of labour develop, whether the worker receives better or worse payment.[34] And after this understanding has more and more made progress in our party, one returns to Lassalle's dogmas, although one must have known that Lassalle *did not know* what wages are, but following in the wake of the bourgeois economists took the appearance for the essence of the matter.

It is as if, among slaves who have at last got behind the secret of slavery and broken out in rebellion, a slave still in thrall to obsolete notions were to inscribe on the programme of the rebellion: Slavery must be abolished because the upkeep of slaves in the system of slavery cannot exceed a certain low maximum!

Does not the mere fact that the representatives of our party were capable of perpetrating such a monstrous attack on the understanding that has spread among the mass of our party, prove by itself with what criminal levity and with what lack of conscience they set to work in drawing up this compromise programme!

Instead of the indefinite concluding phrase of the paragraph—"the removal of all social and political equality"—it ought to have been said that with the abolition of class differences all the social and political inequality arising from them would disappear of itself.

### III.

"The German Workers' Party, in order *to pave the way to the solution of the social question*, demands the establishment of producers' co-operative societies with state aid under the democratic control of the *toiling people*. The producers' co-operative societies *are to be called into being* for industry and agriculture in such dimensions *that the socialist organisation of the total labour will arise from them*."

After the Lassallean "iron law of wages," the remedy of the prophet. The way to it is "paved" in worthy fashion. In place of the existing class struggle appears a newspaper scribbler's phrase: "the social *question*," to the "*solution*" of which one "*paves the way*." Instead of the revolutionary process of transformation of society, the "socialist organisation of the total labour" "arises" from the "state aid" that the state gives to the producers' co-operative societies and which the state, not the worker, "*calls into being*." This is worthy of Lassalle's imagination that one can build a new society by state loans just as well as a new railway!

From the remnants of a sense of shame, "state aid" has been put—under the democratic control of the "toiling people."

In the first place the majority of the "toiling people" in Germany consists of peasants and not of proletarians.

Secondly, "democratic" is in German "*volksherrschaftlich*," ["by the rule of the people"]. But what does "control by the rule of the people of the toiling people" mean? And particularly in the case of a toiling people which, through these demands that it puts to the state, expresses its full consciousness that it neither rules nor is ripe for ruling!

It would be superfluous to deal here with the criticism of the recipe prescribed by Buchez[35] in the reign of Louis Philippe[36] in *opposition* to the French Socialists and accepted by the reactionary workers of the *Atelier*.[37] The chief offence does not lie in having inscribed these specific nostrums in the programme, but in that in general a retrograde step from the standpoint of a class movement to that of a sectarian movement is being taken.

That the workers desire to establish the conditions of co-operative production on a social, and first of all on a national, scale in their own country, only means that they are working to revolutionise the present conditions of production, and has nothing in common with the foundation of co-operative societies with state aid. But as far as the present co-operative societies are concerned they are of value *only* in so far as they are the independent creations of the workers and not protégés either of the government or of the bourgeoisie.

## IV.

I come now to the democratic section.

A. *"The free basis of the state."*

First of all, according to II, the German Workers' Party strives for the "free state."

Free state—what is this?

It is by no means the aim of the workers, who have got rid of the narrow mentality of humble subjects, to set the state free. In the German empire the "state" is almost as "free" as in Russia. Freedom consists in converting the state from an organ standing above society into one completely subordinated to it, and today also the forms of the state are more free or less free to the extent that they restrict the "freedom of the state."

The German Workers' Party—at least if it adopts the programme —shows that its socialist ideas are not even skin-deep, in that, instead of treating existing society (and this holds good of any future one) as the *basis* of the existing state (or of the future state in the case of future society) it treats the state rather as an independent entity that possesses its own *intellectual, moral and free basis*.

And what of the riotous misuse which the programme makes of

the words *"present-day state," "present-day society,"* and of the still more riotous misconception that it achieves in regard to the state to which it addresses its demands?

"Present-day society" is capitalist society, which exists in all civilised countries, more or less free from mediæval admixture, more or less modified by the special historical development of each country and more or less developed. On the other hand, the "present-day state" changes with a country's frontier. It is different in the Prusso-German empire from what it is in Switzerland, it is different in England from what it is in the United States. *"The* present-day state" is therefore a fiction.

Nevertheless, the different states of the different civilised countries, in spite of their manifold diversity of form, all have this in common, that they are based on modern bourgeois society, only one more or less capitalistically developed. They have, therefore, also certain essential features in common. In this sense it is possible to speak of the "present-day state," in contrast to the future in which its present root, bourgeois society, will have died away.

The question then arises: what transformation will the state undergo in communist society? In other words, what social functions will remain in existence there that are analogous to the present functions of the state? This question can only be answered scientifically and one does not get a flea-hop nearer to the problem by a thousand-fold combination of the word people with the word state.

Between capitalist and communist society lies the period of the revolutionary transformation of the one into the other. There corresponds to this also a political transition period in which the state can be nothing but *the revolutionary dictatorship of the proletariat.*[38]

Now the programme does not deal with this nor with the future state in communist society.[39]

Its political demands contain nothing beyond the old familiar democratic litany: universal suffrage, direct legislation, people's justice, a people's militia, etc. They are a mere echo of the bourgeois People's Party,[40] of the League of Peace and Freedom. They are all demands which, in so far as they are not exaggerated in fanciful presentation, have already been *realised.* Only the state to which they belong does not lie within the frontiers of the German empire, but in Switzerland, the United States, etc. This sort of "state of the future" is a present-day state although existing outside the "framework" of the German empire.

But one thing has been forgotten. Since the German Workers' Party expressly declares that it acts within "the present-day national state," hence *its own state*, the Prusso-German empire—its demands would indeed otherwise be largely meaningless, since one only demands what one has not got—it should not have forgotten the chief thing, namely that all those pretty little toys rest on the recognition of the so-called sovereignty of the people and hence there is only room for them in a *democratic republic*.

Since one has not the courage—and wisely, for the circumstances demand caution—to demand the democratic republic, as the French workers' programmes under Louis Philippe and under Louis Napoleon [41] did, one should not have taken refuge either in the subterfuge, neither "honourable" nor "worthy," of demanding things which have meaning only in a democratic republic from a state which is nothing but a police-guarded military despotism, [42] embellished with parliamentary forms, alloyed with a feudal admixture, bureaucratically constructed and already influenced by the bourgeoisie, and then to assure this state into the bargain that one thinks one will be able to extort these things from it "by legal means."

Even vulgar democracy, which sees the millennium in the democratic republic and has no suspicion that it is precisely in this last state form of bourgeois society that the class struggle has to be fought out to a conclusion—even it towers mountains above this kind of democratism within the limits of what is permitted by the police and what is logically impermissible. [43]

That, in fact, by the word "state" the government machinery is understood, or the state in so far as it forms a special organism separated from society through division of labour, is already shown by the words "the German Workers' Party demands *as the economic basis of the state:* a single progressive income tax, etc." Taxes are the economic basis of the government machinery and of nothing else.

In the state of the future as it exists in Switzerland, this demand has been pretty well fulfilled. Income tax presupposes the various sources of income of the various social classes, and hence capitalist society. It is, therefore, not extraordinary that the .Liverpool financial reformers, bourgeois headed by Gladstone's brother,[44] are putting forward the same demand as the programme.

B. "The German Workers' Party demands as the intellectual and moral basis of the state:

1. Universal and *equal elementary education* through the state. Universal compulsory school attendance. Free instruction."

*Equal elementary education?* What idea lies behind these words? Is it believed that in present-day society (and it is only with this one has to deal) education can be *equal* for all classes? Or is it demanded that the upper classes also shall be compulsorily reduced to the modicum of education—the elementary school—that alone is compatible with the economic conditions not only of the wage workers but of the peasants as well.

"Universal compulsory school attendance. Free instruction." The former exists even in Germany, the second in Switzerland and in the United States in the case of elementary schools. If in some states of the latter country the higher educational institutions are also "free," that only means in fact defraying the cost of the education of the upper classes from the general tax receipts. Incidentally, the same holds good for "free administration of justice" demanded under A. 5.* Criminal justice is to be had free everywhere; civil justice is concerned almost exclusively with conflicts over property and hence affects almost exclusively the possessing classes. Should they carry on their litigation at the expense of the national treasury?

The paragraph on the schools should at least have demanded technical schools (theoretical and practical) in combination with the elementary school.

*"Elementary education through the state"* is altogether objectionable. Defining by a general law the financial means of the ele-

---

* Point 5 under A of Section IV of the Programme. See p. 90.—*Ed.*

mentary schools, the qualifications of the teachers, the branches of instruction, etc., and, as happens in the United States, supervising the fulfilment of these legal prescriptions by means of state inspectors, is a very different thing from appointing the state as the educator of the people! Government and church should rather be equally excluded from any influence on the school. Particularly, indeed, in the Prusso-German empire (and one cannot take refuge in the rotten subterfuge that one is speaking of a "state of the future," we have seen what that is) the state has need, on the contrary, of a very stern education by the people.

But the whole programme, for all its democratic clang, is tainted through and through by the servile belief in the state of Lassalle's sect, or, what is no better, by democratic miracle-faith, or rather it is a compromise between these two kinds of miracle-faith, both equally remote from socialism.

*"Freedom of science"* says a paragraph of the Prussian constitution. Why then here?

*"Freedom of conscience"!* If one desires at this time of the *Kulturkampf* [45] to remind liberalism of its old catchwords, then it surely could have been done in the following form: Everyone should be able to attend to his religious as well as his bodily needs without the police sticking their noses in. But the Workers' Party ought at any rate in this connection to have expressed its consciousness of the fact that bourgeois "freedom of conscience" is nothing but the toleration of all possible kinds of *religious freedom of conscience*, and that for its part it endeavours rather to liberate the conscience from the spectre of religion. [46] But there is a desire not to transgress the "bourgeois" level.

I have now come to the end, for the appendix [47] that now follows in the programme does not constitute a characteristic component part of it. Hence I can be very brief here.

## 2. *"Normal working day."*

In no other country has the Workers' Party restricted itself to such an indefinite demand, but has always fixed the length of the working day that it considers normal under the given circumstances.

3. "Restriction of women's labour and prohibition of child labour."

The standardisation of the working day must already include the restriction of women's labour, in so far as it relates to the duration, intervals, etc., of the working day; otherwise it could only mean the exclusion of women's labour from branches of industry that are specifically unhealthy for the female body or are objectionable morally for the female sex. If that is what was meant, then it ought to have been stated.

*"Prohibition of child labour"!* Here it was absolutely essential to state the age limits.

A *general prohibition* of child labour is incompatible with the existence of large-scale industry and hence an empty, pious aspiration.

Its realisation—if it were possible—would be reactionary, since, with a strict regulation of the working time according to the different age groups and other safety measures for the protection of children, an early combination of productive labour with education is one of the most potent means for the transformation of present-day society.

4. "State supervision of factory, workshop and domestic industry."

In regard to the Prusso-German state it should definitely have been demanded that the inspectors are only to be removable by a court of law; that any worker can denounce them to the courts for neglect of duty; that they must belong to the medical profession.

5. "Regulation of prison labour."

A petty demand in a general workers' programme. In any case, it should have been clearly stated that there is no intention from fear of competition to allow ordinary criminals to be treated like beasts, and especially that there is no desire to deprive them of their sole means of betterment, productive labour. This was surely the least one might have expected from socialists.

6. "An effective liability law."

It should have been stated what is understood by an "effective" liability law.

Incidentally, in connection with the normal working day, the part of factory legislation that deals with health regulations and safety measures has been overlooked. The liability law only comes into operation when these regulations are infringed.

In short, this appendix also is distinguished by slovenly editing. *Dixi et salvavi animam meam.*[48]

# APPENDICES

# APPENDIX I

## FROM THE CORRESPONDENCE OF MARX AND ENGELS CONCERNING THE GOTHA PROGRAMME

### FREDERICK ENGELS TO AUGUST BEBEL[49]

London, March 18-28, 1875.

DEAR BEBEL:

I have received your letter of February 23, and am glad you are in such good health.

You ask me what we think of the unification business. Unfortunately our fate has been the same as yours. Neither Liebknecht nor anyone else has sent us any information and we too, therefore, only know what is in the papers, and there was nothing in them until the draft programme appeared about a week ago! This programme has certainly astonished us not a little.

Our party has so frequently made offers of reconciliation or at least of co-operation to the Lassalleans and has been so frequently and contemptuously repulsed by the Hasenclevers, Hasselmanns and Tölckes[50] that any child must have drawn the conclusion: if these gentlemen are now coming and offering reconciliation themselves they must be in a damned tight fix. But considering the well-known character of these people, it is our duty to utilise their fix in order to stipulate for every possible guarantee, so that they shall not re-establish their impaired position in the public opinion of the workers at the expense of our party. They should have been received with extreme coolness and mistrust, and union should have been made dependent on the extent to which they were willing to drop their sectarian slogans and their state aid and to accept in essentials the Eisenach programme of 1869[51] or a revised edition of it adapted to the position at the present day.

27

Our party had *absolutely nothing to learn* from the Lassalleans in the theoretical sphere and therefore in what is decisive for the programme, but the Lassalleans certainly had something to learn from our party; the first condition of union was that they should cease to be sectarians, Lassalleans, above all that the universal panacea of state aid should be, if not entirely relinquished, at any rate recognised by them as a subordinate and transitional measure of less or equal importance to many other possible ones. The draft programme shows that our people are a hundred times superior theoretically to the Lassalleans—but in the same measure removed from being equal to them where political cunning is concerned: the "honest" [52] have been once more cruelly fleeced by the dishonest.

In the first place, Lassalle's high-sounding but historically false phrase is accepted: in contrast to the working class all other classes are only one reactionary mass.[53] This statement is only true in a few exceptional cases: for instance, in a proletarian revolution like the Commune, or in a country where not only have state and society been moulded by the bourgeoisie in its own image but where in its wake the democratic petty bourgeoisie too has already carried out this re-casting down to its final consequences. If in Germany, for instance, the democratic petty bourgeoisie belong to this reactionary mass, how could the Social-Democratic Workers' Party have gone hand in hand with it—with the People's Party—for years? [54] How can the *Volksstaat* [55] take almost the whole of its political contents from the petty-bourgeois democratic *Frankfurter Zeitung?* [56] And how comes it that no less than seven demands are accepted in this programme which directly and literally coincide with the programme of the People's Party and petty-bourgeois democracy? I mean the seven political demands, 1 to 5 and I to II, of which there is not a single one that is not *bourgeois* democratic.[57]

Secondly, the principle that the workers' movement is an international movement is completely disavowed in practice for the present day, and that by people who have upheld this principle in the most glorious way for five years and under the most difficult conditions. The German workers' position at the head of the European movement is *essentially* based on their genuinely international attitude during the war; no other proletariat would have behaved so well.[58] And now this principle is to be denied by them at the very moment when the workers everywhere abroad are emphasising it, in the same degree as the governments are striving to suppress every attempt at its manifestation in an organisation!

And what is left of the internationalism of the workers' movement then? The faint prospect—not even of the future co-operation of the European workers for their emancipation—no, of a future "international brotherhood of nations"—of the bourgeois Peace League's "United States of Europe"!

It was of course quite unnecessary to speak of the International as such. But surely the very least would have been to make no retreat from the programme of 1869 and to say something to this effect: *although* the German Workers' Party is operating *for the time being* within the state boundaries laid down for it (it has no right to speak in the name of the European proletariat and especially no right to say something false), it is conscious of its solidarity with the workers of all countries and will always be ready in the future, as it has been hitherto, to fulfil the obligations imposed upon it by this solidarity. Obligations of that kind exist even if one does not exactly proclaim or regard oneself as a part of the "International"; for instance, help and abstention from blacklegging in strikes; care taken that the party organs keep the German workers informed about the movement abroad; agitation against the threat or the outbreak of Cabinet-made wars, behaviour during such wars similar to that carried out in a model fashion in 1870 and 1871, etc.

Thirdly, our people have allowed the Lassallean "iron law of wages" to be foisted upon them, a law based on a quite antiquated economic view, namely, that the worker receives on the average only the *minimum* of the labour wage, because, according to Malthus' theory of population, there are always too many workers (this was Lassalle's argument). Now Marx has proved in detail in *Capital* that the laws regulating wages are very complicated, that sometimes one predominates and sometimes another, according to circumstances, that therefore they are in no sense iron but on the contrary very elastic, and that the thing can by no means be dismissed in a few words, as Lassalle imagined. The Malthusian basis for the law which Lassalle copied from Malthus and Ricardo (with a falsification of the latter), as it is to be found, for instance, in the *Arbeiterlesebuch*, page 5, quoted from another pamphlet of Lassalle's,[59] has been refuted in detail by Marx in the section on the "Accumulation of Capital." Thus by adopting Lassalle's "iron law" we commit ourselves to a false statement with a false basis.

Fourthly, the programme puts forward as its *sole social* demand —Lassalle's state aid in its most naked form, as Lassalle stole it from Buchez. And this after Bracke[60] has very well exposed this demand in its entire nullity and after almost all, if not all, our party speakers have been obliged to come out against this state aid in fighting the Lassalleans! Lower than this our party could not abase itself. Internationalism brought down to Amand Gögg[61] and socialism to the bourgeois republican Buchez, who put forward this demand *in opposition to the socialists,* in order to supplant them!

In the best of cases, however, "state aid" in the Lassallean sense is only one *particular* measure among many others designed to attain the end here lamely described as "paving the way to a solution of the social question"—as if a theoretically *unsolved* social *question* still existed for us! So if we say: the German Workers' Party strives for the abolition of wage labour, and with it of class differences, by the establishment of co-operative production on a national scale in industry and agriculture; it supports every measure adapted to the attainment of this end!—then no Lassallean can have anything against it.

Fifthly, there is not a word about the organisation of the working class as a class by means of the trade unions. And that is a very essential point, for this is the real class organisation of the proletariat, in which it carries on its daily struggles with capital, in which it trains itself, and which nowadays even amid the worst reaction (as in Paris at present) can simply no longer be smashed. Considering the importance which this form of organisation has also attained in Germany, it would be absolutely necessary in our opinion to mention it in the programme and if possible to leave open a place for it in the party organisation.

All this has been done by our people to please the Lassalleans. And what has the other side conceded? That a crowd of rather confused *purely democratic demands* should figure in the programme, of which several are a mere matter of fashion, as for instance the "legislation by the people" which exists in Switzerland and does more harm than good when it does anything at all. *Administration* by the people would be something different. Equally lacking is the first condition of all freedom: that all functionaries should be responsible for all their official actions to every citizen before the ordinary courts and according to common law. Of the fact that such demands as freedom for science, freedom of conscience, figure in every bourgeois liberal programme and have a somewhat strange appearance here, I will say nothing more.

The free people's state is transformed into the free state. Taken in its grammatical sense a free state is one where the state is free in relation to its citizens and is therefore a state with a despotic government. The whole talk about the state should be dropped, especially since the Commune, which was no longer a state in the proper sense of the word. The *"people's state"* has been thrown in our faces by the anarchists too long, although Marx's book against Proudhon [62] and later *The Communist Manifesto* [63] directly declare that with the introduction of the socialist order of society the state will of itself dissolve and disappear. As, therefore, the "state" is only a transitory institution which is used in the struggle, in the revolution, in order to hold down [*niederzuhalten*] one's adversaries by force, it is pure nonsense to talk of a "free people's state"; so long as the proletariat still *uses* the state, it does not use it in the interests of freedom but in order to hold down its adversaries, and as soon as it becomes possible to speak of freedom, the state as such ceases to exist. [64] We would therefore propose to replace the word *"state"* everywhere by the word *Gemeinwesen* [community], a good old German word, which can very well represent the French word *commune*. [65]

"The removal of all social and political inequality" is also a very questionable phrase in place of "the abolition of all class differences." Between one country and another, one province and another and even one place and another, there will always exist a *certain* inequality in the conditions of life, which can be reduced to a minimum but never entirely removed. Mountain dwellers will always have different conditions of life from those of people living on plains. The idea of socialist society as the realm of equality is a one-sided French idea resting upon the old "liberty, equality, fraternity"—an idea which was justified as a *stage of development* in its own time and place, but which, like all the one-sided ideas of the earlier socialist schools, should now be overcome, for they only produce confusion in people's heads and more precise modes of presentation have been found.

I will stop, although almost every word in this programme, which has, moreover, been put together in a flat and feeble style, could be criticised. It is of such a character that if it is accepted Marx and I can *never* give our adherence to the *new* party established on this basis, and shall have very seriously to consider what our attitude towards it—in public as well—[66] should be. You must remember that abroad *we* are made responsible for any and every utterance and action of the German Social-Democratic Workers' Party. Thus Bakunin in his pamphlet, *Statehood and Anarchy*[67]—where we have to answer for every thoughtless word spoken or written by Liebknecht[68] since the *Demokratisches Wochenblatt*[69] was started. People imagine, indeed, that we issue our orders for the whole business from here, while you know as well as I that we hardly ever interfere in internal party affairs in the smallest way, and even then only in order to make good, so far as is possible, blunders, and only theoretical blunders, which have in our opinion been committed. But you will see for yourself that this programme marks a turning point which may very easily compel us to refuse any and every responsibility for the party which recognises it.

As a rule, the official programme of a party is less important than what it does. But a *new* programme is after all a banner publicly raised, and the outside world judges the party from it. It should therefore on no account include a step backwards, as this one does in comparison with the Eisenach programme. One should surely also take into consideration what the workers of other countries will say to this programme, what impression will be produced by this bending of the knee to Lassalleanism on the part of the whole German socialist proletariat.

At the same time I am convinced that a union on *this* basis will never last a year. Are the best minds in our party to lend themselves to grinding out repetitions, learnt by rote, of the Lassallean statements on the iron law of wages and state aid? I should like to see you doing it, for instance! And if they did do this they would be hissed by their audiences. And I am sure the Lassalleans will insist on just *these* points of their programme like the Jew Shylock on his pound of flesh. The separation will come; but we shall have "rehabilitated" Hasselmann, Hasenclever, Tölcke and Co.; we shall come out of the separation weaker and the Lassalleans stronger; our party will have lost its political virginity and will never again be able to come out whole-heartedly against the Lassallean phrases which it will have inscribed for a time on its own banner; and if the Lassalleans then once more say that they are the most genuine, the only workers' party, while our people are bourgeois, the programme will be there to prove it. All the socialist measures in it are *theirs,* and all *our* party has put into it are the demands of that same petty-bourgeois democracy which is nevertheless *also* described *by it* in the same programme as a part of the "reactionary mass."

I had left this letter lying as after all you are to be freed on April 1 in honour of Bismarck's birthday,[70] and I did not want to expose it to the chance of being seized in any attempt to smuggle it in. And now a letter has just come from Bracke, who has also his grave doubts about the programme and wants to know our opinion.[71] I am therefore sending this letter to him to forward, so that he can read it and so that I need not write out all this stuff over again. Moreover, I have also told the unvarnished truth to Ramm[72]— to Liebknecht I only wrote briefly. I cannot forgive him for never telling us a *single word* about the thing (while Ramm and others thought he had given us exact information) until it was too late, so to speak. But indeed this is what he has always done—hence the large amount of disagreeable correspondence which both Marx and I have had with him, but this time it is really too much and *we are certainly not going to co-operate.*

See that you contrive to come here in the summer. You will, of course, stay with me, and if the weather is good we can go to the seaside for a day or two, which will be really beneficial to you after your long spell in jail.

Your sincere friend,

F. E.

### KARL MARX TO WILHELM BRACKE [73]

London, May 5, 1875.

DEAR BRACKE:

When you have read the following critical marginal notes on the Unity Programme, would you be so good as to send them to Geib and Auer,[74] Bebel and Liebknecht for them to see? I am excessively busy and have already had to go a long way beyond the extent of work allowed me by the doctor. Hence it was anything but a "pleasure" to write such a lengthy screed. It was, however, necessary so that the steps that have to be taken by me later on will not be misinterpreted by our friends in the party for whom this communication is intended. After the Unity Congress has been held, Engels and I will publish a short declaration to the effect that our position is altogether remote from the said programme of principles and that we have nothing to do with it.

This is indispensable because the opinion—the entirely erroneous opinion—is held abroad, assiduously nurtured by enemies of the party, that we secretly guide from here the movements of the so-called Eisenach party. In a Russian pamphlet that has recently appeared,[75] Bakunin again makes me responsible, for example, not only for all the programmes, etc., of that party but even for every step taken by Liebknecht from the day of his co-operation with the People's Party.

Apart from this, it is my duty not to give recognition, even by diplomatic silence, to what is in my opinion a thoroughly objectionable programme tending to demoralise the party.

Every step of real movement is more important than a dozen programmes. If, therefore, it was not possible—and the conditions of the time did not permit it—to go *beyond* the Eisenach programme, one should simply have concluded an agreement for action against the common enemy. But by drawing up a programme of principles (instead of postponing this until it has been prepared for by a considerable period of common activity) one sets up before the whole world a landmark by which the level of the party movement is measured. The Lassallean leaders came because circumstances forced them to come. If they had been told from the beginning that there would be no bargaining about principles, they would have *had* to be content with a programme of action or a plan of organisation for common action. Instead of this, they have been permitted to arrive armed with mandates, these mandates have been recognised on our part as valid, and thus one surrenders unconditionally to those who are in need of help. To crown the whole business, they are holding a congress again *before the Congress of Compromise,* while our own party is holding its congress *post festum.*[76] There has obviously been a desire to stifle all criticism and to prevent our own party from considering the matter. One knows that the mere fact of unification is satisfying to the workers, but it would be a mistake to believe that this immediate success is not being bought at too high a price.

For the rest, the programme is no good, even apart from its sanctification of the Lassallean articles of faith.

I shall be sending you in the near future the last parts of the French edition of *Capital.* The progress of the printing was held up for a considerable time owing to the ban of the French government. The thing will be ready this week or the end of next week.[77] Have you received the previous six parts? Please let me have the address of Bernhard Becker [78] to whom I must also send the final parts.

The bookshop of the *Volksstaat* has its own way of behaving. Up to this moment, for example, I have not been sent a single copy of the publication on the Cologne Communist Trial.[79]

With best wishes,

Yours,

KARL MARX

## FREDERICK ENGELS TO WILHELM BRACKE

London, October 11, 1875.

DEAR BRACKE:

I have delayed answering your last letters (the last being June 28) up to now, first because Marx and I were separated for six weeks—he was in Carlsbad and I was at the seaside, where I did not see the *Volksstaat*—and then, because I wanted to wait a little to see how the new unification and the combined committee [80] would behave in practice.

We are entirely of your opinion that Liebknecht, in his zeal to obtain the unification and to pay *any* price for it, has muddled the whole business. It was possible to consider that necessary, but there was no need to say so to the other contracting party or to show it. Afterwards, one mistake has always to be justified by another. After the Unity Congress had once been set on foot on a rotten basis and trumpeted abroad, it could not be allowed to fail at any price and thus one had afresh to give way in essential points. You are quite right: this unification bears the seeds of a split within itself, and I shall be glad if then *only* the incurable fanatics fall away and not also an entire following, otherwise vigorous and, under good instruction, possible to make use of. That will depend on the time when, and the circumstances in which, the inevitable takes place.

The programme in its final form consists of three component parts:

1. Of the Lassallean phrases and catchwords, which could not be accepted on any condition. If two fractions unite, one puts in the programme what one is in agreement upon, not what is in dispute. But, in that they allowed this, our people voluntarily went through the Caudine Forks.*

2. A series of vulgar democratic demands, set out in the spirit and style of the People's Party.

---

* A narrow valley in Italy where the Romans were disastrously defeated by the Samnites in 321 B.C. As a result, the Roman commanders had to accept humiliating conditions of peace.—*Ed.*

3. A series of would-be communist propositions, mostly borrowed from the *Manifesto* but so re-edited that looked at closely, one and all are seen to contain hair-raising nonsense. If one does not understand these matters, one should keep one's fingers off them, or copy them literally from those who admittedly do understand the thing.

Fortunately, the programme has fared better than it deserves. Both workers and bourgeois and petty bourgeois read into it what ought properly to be in it but is not in it, and it has not occurred to anyone to investigate publicly a single one of these wonderful propositions as to its real content. This has made it possible for us to keep silent on this programme. It comes to this, that one cannot translate these propositions into any foreign language without being *compelled* either to write down palpably crazy stuff or to insert a communist meaning into them, and the latter has been done so far by friend and foe. I myself have had to do so in a translation for our Spanish friends.

What I have seen of the activity of the committee is so far not encouraging. First, the attack on your and B. Becker's writings; [81] it was not the fault of the committee that it did not go through. Secondly, Sonnemann,[82] whom Marx saw on his journey through, reported that he had offered Vahlteich [83] some correspondence for the *Frankfurter Zeitung*, but that the committee had *forbidden* Vahlteich to accept it! That surely exceeds even the censorship and I cannot conceive how Vahlteich could allow such a thing to be forbidden him. And the clumsiness of it! They should rather have taken care that everywhere in Germany the *Frankfurter Zeitung* should be served by our people! Finally, the procedure of the Lassallean members on the foundation of the Berlin printing house of the Association does also not appear to me to be very honest; while our people, in the case of the Leipzig printing house, had in all confidence appointed the committee as the supervisory council, those in Berlin had to be *compelled* to do so. However, I do not know the details here exactly.

Meanwhile it is good that the committee is displaying little activity and confines itself, as K. Hirsch,[84] who was here in recent days, says, to vegetating as a correspondence and information bureau.

Any vigorous intervention on its part would only hasten the crisis and the people seem to sense this.

And what weakness, to accept three Lassalleans and two of our people on the committee! [85]

Altogether, we seem to have come off with a black eye, and a big one at that. Let us hope that it rests at that, and that in the meantime the propaganda has its effect among the Lassalleans. If the thing lasts until the next Reichstag elections, it can be all right. But then Stieber [86] and Tessendorf [87] would do their best, and then the time will also come when it will be seen *what* has been taken over in Hasselmann and Hasenclever.

Marx has come back from Carlsbad quite changed, vigorous, fresh, cheerful and healthy, and can soon get down seriously to work again. He and I send you hearty greetings. When you have a chance let us hear from you again how the business goes. The Leipzigers [88] are all too deeply interested in it to tell us the real truth and the *internal* party history particularly just now does not get made public.

Yours very sincerely,

F. E.

### FREDERICK ENGELS TO AUGUST BEBEL

London, October 12, 1875.

DEAR BEBEL:

Your letter fully confirms our view that the unification is premature on our part and bears within it the seeds of future conflict. If one succeeds in postponing this conflict until after the next Reichstag elections,[89] that would already be good. . . .

The programme, as it is now, consists of the following parts:

1. Of the Lassallean propositions and catchwords, to have accepted which remains a disgrace for our party. If two fractions unite on a programme, they put in the things on which they agree and do not touch on what they are not agreed. It is true that Lassalle's state aid stood in the Eisenach programme,[90] but as *one* of many *transitional measures*, and, according to all that I have heard, it was

fairly certain, *without* the unification, to have been thrown out on Bracke's[91] motion in this year's congress. Now it figures as the one infallible and exclusive remedy for all social crimes. To have allowed the "iron law of wages" and other Lassallean phrases to be foisted on one was a colossal moral defeat for our party. The party became converted to the Lassallean confession of faith. That is simply not to be denied away. This part of the programme is the Caudine Forks through which our party has crawled to the greater glory of Saint Lassalle.

2. Of democratic demands, which are set out entirely in the sense and in the style of the People's Party.

3. Of demands addressed to the *"present-day state"* (from which it is not known to whom the other "demands" are addressed) which are very confused and illogical.

4. Of general propositions, mostly borrowed from *The Communist Manifesto* and the Statutes of the International, but which have been so edited that they contain either *total falsehood* or *pure nonsense,* as Marx proved in the essay well known to you.[92]

The whole is in the highest degree disorderly, confused, unconnected, illogical and discreditable. If there had been a single critical mind in the bourgeois press, he would have gone through this programme sentence by sentence, investigated each sentence in respect to its real content, set out the nonsense in a properly palpable way, analysed the contradictions and economic howlers (*e.g.,* that the instruments of labour are today the "monopoly of the capitalist class," as if there were no landowners, the talk of "emancipation of *labour*" instead of the working class, labour itself is nowadays indeed *much too free!*) and made our party extremely ridiculous. Instead of that, the asses of the bourgeois papers have taken this programme quite seriously, have read into it what is not there and interpreted it in a communist sense. The workers appear to do the same. It is *this circumstance alone* which has made it possible for Marx and myself not to dissociate ourselves publicly from such a programme. So long as our opponents and the workers likewise insert our views into this programme it is permissible for us to keep silent about it.

If you are content with the result in the question of persons, then the claims on our side must have sunk pretty low. Two of our people and three Lassalleans! Thus, here also our people are not allies with equal rights but the vanquished and the outvoted from the start. The actions of the committee, so far as we know them, are also not edifying: 1. resolved *not* to put Bracke's and B. Becker's two works on Lassalleanism on the list of party publications; if this has been withdrawn it is neither the fault of the executive committee nor of Liebknecht; 2. the forbidding of Vahlteich to accept the correspondence offered him by Sonnemann for the *Frankfurter Zeitung*. This, Sonnemann told Marx himself when the latter was on his journey. What surprises me in this even more than the arrogance of the committee, and the readiness with which Vahlteich has complied instead of flouting the committee, is the colossal stupidity of this resolution. The committee ought rather to have taken care that a paper like the *Frankfurter Zeitung* should everywhere be served *only* by our people.[93]

. . . That the whole thing is an educational experiment which even under these circumstances promises a very favourable result, in that you are quite right. The unification as such is a great success, if it lasts for two years! But it was undoubtedly to be had far more cheaply.

F. E.

### FOREWORD BY FREDERICK ENGELS TO THE "CRITIQUE OF THE GOTHA PROGRAMME"[94]

The manuscript published here—the covering letter to Bracke[95] as well as the critique of the draft programme—was sent in 1875, shortly before the Gotha Unity Congress, to Bracke for communication to Geib, Auer, Bebel and Liebknecht and subsequent return to Marx. Since the Halle Party Congress[96] has put the discussion of the Gotha Programme on the agenda of the party, I think I would be guilty of suppression if I any longer withheld from publicity this important—perhaps the most important—document relevant to this discussion.

But the manuscript has yet another and more far-reaching significance. Here for the first time Marx's attitude to the line adopted by Lassalle since the latter embarked on his agitation is clearly and firmly formulated, both as regards Lassalle's economic principles and his tactics.

The ruthless severity with which the draft programme is dissected here, the mercilessness with which the results obtained are enunciated and the shortcomings of the draft laid bare, all this today, after fifteen years, can no longer give offence. Specific Lassalleans now only exist abroad as isolated ruins and in Halle the Gotha Programme has been given up even by its creators as altogether inadequate.

Nevertheless, I have omitted a few sharp personal expressions and judgments, where these were of no importance to the matter, and replaced them by dots. Marx himself would have done so if he had published the manuscript today. The violence of the language in some passages was provoked by two circumstances. In the first instance, Marx and I had been more intimately connected with the German movement than with any other; we were, therefore, bound to be particularly intensely perturbed by the decidedly retrograde step manifested by this draft programme. And secondly, we were at that time, hardly two years after the Hague Congress of the International,[97] engaged in the most violent struggle against Bakunin and his anarchists[98] who made us responsible for everything that happened in the labour movement in Germany; hence we had to expect that we would also be saddled with the secret paternity of this programme. These considerations do not now exist and so there is no necessity for the passages in question.

For reasons arising from the Press Law, also, a few sentences have been only indicated by dots. Where I have had to choose a milder expression this has been enclosed in square brackets.[99] Otherwise the text has been published word for word.

F. ENGELS

London, January 6, 1891.

## FREDERICK ENGELS TO KARL KAUTSKY[100]

London, February 23, 1891.

DEAR KAUTSKY:

You will have received my hasty congratulations of the day before yesterday. So now to return again to our muttons, the Marx letter.

The fear that it would put a weapon in the hands of our opponents was unfounded. Malicious insinuations, of course, are being attached to everything and anything, but on the whole the impression made on the opponents was one of complete disconcertion at this ruthless self-criticism and the feeling, what an inner power must be possessed by a party that can afford such a thing! That can be seen from the hostile newspapers that you sent me (for which many thanks) and from those to which I have otherwise had access. And, frankly speaking, that was also my intention when I published the document. That at the first moment some persons here and there could not but be unpleasantly affected by it, of that I was aware, but it was not to be avoided and it was amply outweighed in my view by the material contents. I knew, also, that the party was fully strong enough to bear it, and I reckoned that it would today also put up with this frank language used fifteen years ago, that it would point with justifiable pride to this test of strength and would say: Where is there another party that can dare the like? That has been left, meanwhile, to the *Sächsischer* and *Wiener Arbeiter-Zeitung* and to the *Züricher Post*.[101]

That in No. 21 of the *Neue Zeit* you take on yourself the responsibility for the publication is very gallant of you, but do not forget that, after all, I gave the first impulse and moreover to a certain extent I put you in a position in which you had no choice.[102] I claim, therefore, the main responsibility for myself. As far as details are concerned, one can certainly always have different opinions about them. I have deleted and altered everything that you and Dietz[103] have objected to, and if Dietz had marked even more I would still, as far as possible, have been amenable even then, of that I have always given you proof. But, as far as the main point is concerned, it was *my duty* to publish the thing when once the programme had come up for discussion. And especially now, after Liebknecht's report in Halle, in which he utilises his extracts from it, in part unceremoniously as his own property, and in part on the other hand as objects of attack without mentioning the source,[104] Marx would certainly have confronted this version with the original and it was my duty in his place to do the same. Unfortunately, at that time I had not yet got the document. I only found it later after much search.

You say that Bebel[105] writes to you that Marx's treatment of Lassalle has caused bad blood among the old Lassalleans. That may be. People do not know the real story and nothing appears to have happened to enlighten them about it.[106] If these people do not know that Lassalle's whole greatness rests on this, that for years Marx allowed him to parade the results of Marx's research as his own and, owing to defective education in economics, to distort them into the bargain, then that is not my fault. But I am Marx's literary executor and as such I also have my duty to perform.

Lassalle has belonged to history for twenty-six years. While under the Exceptional Law historical criticism of him has been left in abeyance, the time is at last at hand when it must have its say and Lassalle's position in relation to Marx be made clear. The legend that conceals and glorifies the true stature of Lassalle cannot become an article of faith of the party. However highly one may estimate Lassalle's services to the movement, his historical role in it remains an equivocal one. Lassalle the socialist is accompanied step by step by Lassalle the demagogue. Lassalle, the conductor of the Hatzfeld law suit,[107] appears everywhere, showing through Lassalle the agitator and organiser; the same cynicism in choice of methods, the same preference for surrounding himself with rowdy and corrupt people who can be used as mere tools and discarded. Until 1862, a specifically Prussian vulgar democrat in practice, with strong Bonapartist leanings (I have just looked through his letters to Marx), he suddenly turned round from purely personal causes and began his agitation; and before two years had gone by he was demanding that the workers should take the part of the monarchy against the bourgeoisie, and intriguing with Bismarck, one of his own kin in character, in a way that was bound to lead to the actual betrayal of the movement, if fortunately for him he had not been shot in time. In his agitational writings, the correct things that he borrowed from Marx are so much interwoven with his own invariably false expositions that the two are hardly to be separated. The section of the workers that feels itself injured by Marx's judgment only knows Lassalle through his two years of agitation, and they also see them through coloured spectacles. But historical criticism cannot stand eternally, hat in hand, before such prejudices. It was my duty finally to settle accounts between Marx and Lassalle. That has been done. For the time being I can content myself with that. Moreover, I myself have other things to do now. And the published ruthless judgment of Marx on Lassalle will by itself have its effect and give others courage. But should I be forced to it, there would be no choice for me; I should have to clear away the Lassalle legend once for all.

That voices have been raised in the fraction saying that the *Neue Zeit* should be placed under censorship is indeed a fine affair. Is the ghost of the fraction's dictatorship during the Anti-Socialist Law (which was of course necessary and excellently carried out) [108] now appearing, or is it due to remembrance of the late strict organisation of Schweitzer? [109] It is in fact a brilliant idea to put German socialist science, after its liberation from Bismarck's Anti-Socialist Law, under a new socialist law manufactured and carried out by the Social Democratic Party officials themselves. For the rest, it is ordained that the desires of the ambitious will not be realised.

The article in the *Vorwärts* does not stir me much.[110] I shall wait for Liebknecht's historical account [111] and shall then reply to both in as friendly a tone as possible. In the *Vorwärts* article there are only a few inaccuracies to be corrected (*e.g.*, that we did not desire unity, that events proved Marx wrong, etc.) and a few obvious things to be confirmed. With this answer I intend then, for my part, to close the discussion unless new attacks or false assertions compel me to continue.

Tell Dietz that I am working on the *Origin* [112] but today Fischer [113] writes to me and wants three new prefaces as well! [114]

Yours,

F. E.

9049

Address

Sold to

Date _____ 19___

"EGGS FROM HEN TO YOU"

Yorktown Heights, N. Y. • YO 2-4000

Gomer St. • R.D. 2 • Box 2027

# GOMER POULTRY FARM

# APPENDIX II

## LENIN ON THE *CRITIQUE OF THE GOTHA PROGRAMME*

### FROM HIS NOTEBOOK *MARXISM ON THE STATE*

(January-February 1917)

### ENGELS' LETTER TO BEBEL

**Engels'** letter to *Bebel* of 18-28, III, 1875, is of *exceptionally* great importance on the question of the state. (Bebel, *From My Life,* Vol. II, p. 318 and the following pages. Stuttgart, 1911; preface of 2, IX, 1911.)

Here is the most important passage in full: ". . . The free people's state is transformed into the free state. Taken in its grammatical sense a free state is one where the state is free in relation to its citizens and is therefore a state with a despotic government. **The whole talk about the state should be dropped,** especially *since the Commune,* **which was no longer a state in the proper sense of the word.** The *'people's state'* has been thrown in our faces by the anarchists too long, although Marx's book against Proudhon and later *The Communist Manifesto* directly declare that *with the introduction of the socialist order of society* **the state will of itself dissolve and disappear.** As, therefore, the 'state' is only a transitory institution which is used in the

NB

47

struggle, in the revolution, in order to hold down one's adversaries by force, it is pure nonsense to talk of a 'free people's state'; so long as the proletariat still *uses* (Engels' italics) the state, it does *not* use it *in the interests of freedom but in order to hold down its adversaries, and as soon as it becomes possible to speak of freedom, the state as such ceases to exist.* We would therefore propose to replace the word *'state'* (Engels' italics) everywhere by the word *Gemeinwesen* [community],* a good old German word, which can very well represent the French word *commune.*" (Pp. 321-22.)

NB

NB

This is probably the most striking and certainly the sharpest passage, so to speak, "*against* the state," in Marx and Engels.

(1) "The whole talk about the state should be dropped."

(2) "The Commune was no longer a state in the proper sense of the word." (But what, then? A transitional form from the state to no state, clearly!)

(3) The anarchists have long enough "thrown in our faces" the "people's state." (Marx and Engels, it is clear, were ashamed of this obvious mistake on the part of their German friends;—however, they thought, and of course *under the circumstances* **then existing** rightly thought, that it was an incomparably less serious mistake than the mistake of the anarchists. N.B. this!!)

(4) The state "will of itself decompose ("dissolve") ⸤ *Nota bene* ⸥ and disappear. . ." (compare further on "will wither away")

* Lenin uses here the Russian word, *obshchina.—Ed.*

"with the introduction of the socialist order of society. . . ."

(5) The state is "a temporary institution," which is needed "in the struggle, in the revolution . . ." (needed *by the proletariat,* of course). . . .

(6) The state is needed *not for freedom,* but for *crushing* (?*Niederhaltung* is not holding down, properly speaking, but holding back from restoration, holding in submission) *the adversaries of the proletariat.*

(7) When there is freedom, then there will be no state.

---

The concepts "freedom" and "democracy" are usually considered as identical and are often used instead of each other. Very often the vulgar Marxists (with Kautsky, Plekhanov and Co. at their head) have precisely this conception. In fact, democracy excludes freedom. The dialectics (process) of development is: from absolutism to bourgeois democracy; from bourgeois democracy to proletarian; from proletarian to none at all.

---

(8) "We" (*i.e.,* Engels and *Marx*) would propose *"everywhere"* (in the programme) to speak, instead of the "state," of the "community," the "commune"!!!      **NB!!!!**

From this it is clear how not only the opportunists, but also Kautsky, have vulgarised, defiled Marx and Engels.

The opportunists have *not* understood a single one of these *eight* most rich ideas!!

They have taken *only* the practical needs of the present: to make use of the political struggle, to make use of the *contemporary* state for the training, the education of the proletariat, for the "extraction of concessions." This is correct (as against the anarchists), but as yet it is only one one-hundredth of Marxism, if it can be so arithmetically expressed.

Kautsky completely covered over (or forgot? or did not understand?), in his propagandist and throughout his publicist work, points 1, 2, 5, 6, 7, 8, and Marx's "smashing" (in his polemic with Pannekoek in 1912 or 1913 * Kautsky has already tumbled completely into opportunism on this question).

We are distinguished from the anarchists by ($\alpha$) utilisation of the state *now* and ($\beta$) at the time of the proletarian *revolution* ("the dictatorship of the proletariat")—points of the greatest practical importance, at this very moment. (And it is these that Bukharin *has forgotten*!)

From the opportunists by the deeper, "more eternal," truth concerning ($\alpha\alpha$) the "temporary" character of the state, ($\beta\beta$) the *harm* of "chatter" about it now, ($\gamma\gamma$) the dictatorship of the proletariat not having altogether the character of the state, ($\delta\delta$) the contradiction between the state and freedom, ($\varepsilon\varepsilon$) the greater correctness of the idea (conception, programme term) "community" in place of state, (ςς) the "smashing" of the bureaucratic-military machine. Not to forget also that the *dictatorship of the proletariat* is di-

* See Lenin, *State and Revolution*, pp. 93-100—*Ed.*

rectly repudiated by the avowed opportunists of Germany (Bernstein, Kolb and so forth), and *indirectly* by the official programme and Kautsky, being silent about it in everyday agitation, and *tolerating* the renegacy of the Kolbs and Co.

Bukharin was written to in VIII. 1916: "Let your ideas on the state *ripen fully.*" But *without letting them* ripen, he rushed into print as "Nota bene," and he did it in such a way that instead of exposing the Kautsky-ans he *helped* them by his own mistakes!! But in the essence of the matter Bukharin is nearer to the truth than Kautsky.

*Neue Zeit* XIX, I (1900-1901) (No. 26, 27. III. 1901) p. 804: **M. Beer** on the decline of England with notes on her imperialism, *decay,* and the *imperialism* of other countries. ———NB the same author: "Social Imperialism," *Neue Zeit* XX, I (1901-1902) pp. 209 and following (the Fabians) and "The Present Position of Trade Unionism," *same,* p. 43 (NB) ((*"The Imperialist-Social Era"*)).

XIX, 2, p. 197: *Walter's* article on "Russian Imperialism". . . ((from Peter I to *China* in the XXth century)).

|| NB

## MARX: "CRITIQUE OF THE GOTHA PROGRAMME"

*Engels'* letter *to Bebel* was written 28.III. 1875. *Marx's* letter to Bracke *with the Critique of the Gotha Programme was written* more than a month later: 5. V. 1875. (*Neue Zeit* IX, 1; 1891.) (*1890-1891, No. 18.*)

At first glance Marx in this letter looks much more like "an adherent of the state"—if it is permissible to use this insipid expression of our adversaries—than Engels.

Engels proposes (1) not to speak of the state at all; (2) to replace this word with "community"; (3) he declares even the Commune (*i.e.*, "the dictatorship of the proletariat") "no longer a state in the proper sense of the word,"—while Marx says *not a whisper* on all this, *but on the contrary,* even speaks of the "future *state organisation* of communist society"!! (*Neue Zeit* IX, 1, p. 573.)

!!

At first glance the impression may be obtained that there is flat contradiction, confusion or divergence of view! But that is only at first glance.

Here in full is the decisive (on this point) passage from Marx's letter:

" 'Present-day society' is capitalist society, which exists in all civilised countries, more or less free from mediæval admixture, more or less modified by the special historical development of each country and more or less developed. On the other hand, the 'present-day state' changes with a country's frontier. It is different in the Prusso-German empire from what it is in Switzerland, it is different in England from what it is in the United States. '*The* present-day state' is therefore a fiction.

"Nevertheless, the different states of the different civilised countries, in spite of their manifold diversity of form, all have this in common, that they are based on modern bour-

geois society, only one more or less capitalistically developed. They have, therefore, also
certain essential features in common. In this
sense it is possible to speak of the 'present-
day state,' in contrast to the future in which its
present root, bourgeois society, will have died
away.

"The question then arises: what transformation will the **state** undergo *in communist
society?* In other words, *what social functions will remain in existence there that are
analogous to the present functions of the
state?* This question can only be answered
scientifically and one does not get a flea-hop
nearer to the problem by a thousand-fold
combination of the word people with the
word state.

"Between capitalist and communist society
lies the period of the revolutionary transformation of the one into the other. There
corresponds to this also a political transition
period in which the state can be nothing but
*the revolutionary dictatorship of the prole-
tariat.* (Marx's italics.) (Pp. 572-73.)

"Now the programme does not deal with
this nor *with the future state in communist
society.*

NB

It is clear that this is a rebuke; this
is clear from the following phrase: the
programme "deals" with the old democratic litany, *but not* with the questions
of the revolutionary dictatorship of the
proletariat and the stat~ in communist
society. . . .

"Its political demands contain nothing beyond the old familiar democratic litany: universal suffrage, direct legislation, people's justice, a people's militia, etc. They are a mere echo of the bourgeois People's Party, of the League of Peace and Freedom. . . ." (P. 573.)

(These demands are already "realised"—only not in the German state, but in others, in Switzerland, in the United States. These demands are in place *only* in a *democratic republic*. The programme does not demand a republic, as the French workers' programme did under Louis Philippe and Louis Napoleon—this is impossible in Germany, hence it is useless to demand things, which are in place only in a democratic republic, from a military despotism . . . even vulgar democracy *"towers mountains above this kind of democratism within the limits of what is permitted by the police and what is logically impermissible."*)

very good (and very important)

In these words Marx as it were foresaw the whole banality of Kautskyanism: sweet speeches about all kinds of fine things, turning into the beautifying of reality, because they shade over or leave in the dark the irreconcilability of democratic peace and imperialism, of democracy and monarchy, etc.

Thus, the dictatorship of the proletariat is a "political transition period"; it is clear that also *the state of this period* is a transition from the state to no state, *i.e.*, "no longer a state in the proper sense of the word." Marx and Engels, therefore, do not in any way contradict each other on this point.

But further on Marx speaks of "the future state of communist society"!! Thus, even in *communist* society the state will exist!! Is there not a contradiction in this?

No!   I — — in capitalist society, a state in the proper sense of the word

the state is needed by the bourgeoisie

II — — the transition (dictatorship of the proletariat) a state of the transitional type (not a state in the proper sense of the word)

the state is needed by the proletariat

III — — communist society: *the with-ering away* of the state.

the state is not needed, it withers away

Complete consistency and clarity!!
In other words:

I — Democracy only by way of exception, and never complete. . . .

I — Democracy only for the rich and for a small layer of the proletariat. [It is not for the poor man!]

II — Democracy almost complete, limited only by the *crushing* of the resistance of the bourgeoisie.

II — Democracy for the poor, for $\frac{9}{10}$ of the population, crushing of the resistance of the rich by force.

III — Democracy really complete, becoming a habit and *for that reason* withering away. . . . Complete democracy equals no democracy. This is not a paradox, but a truth!

III — Democracy complete, becoming a habit and for that reason withering away, giving place to the principle: "From each according to his ability, to each according to his needs."

See p. 19 marginal note. | *

The question of the state is also referred to in the very vital passage of the *Critique of the Gotha Programme* devoted to the *economic* analysis of future society.

Marx here (pp. 565-67) criticises the Lassallean idea of "the undiminished proceeds of labour," shows the need to set aside a fund to cover the wearing out of part of the means of production, a reserve fund, the costs of administration, of schools, health services and so forth, *and continues:*

"What we have to deal with here is a communist society, not as it has *developed* on its own foundations, but, on the contrary, as it *emerges* from capitalist society; which is thus in every respect, economically, morally and intellectually, still stamped with the birthmarks of the old society from whose womb it

NB

* See p. 58.—*Ed.*

emerges. Accordingly the individual producer receives back from society—after the deductions have been made—exactly what he gives to it. What he has given to it is his individual amount of labour. For example, the social working day consists of the sum of the individual labour hours; the individual labour time of the individual producer is the part of the social labour day contributed by him, his share in it. He receives a certificate from society that he has furnished such and such an amount of labour (after deducting his labour for the common fund), and with this certificate he draws from the social stock of means of consumption as much as the same amount of labour costs. The same amount of labour which he has given to society in one form, he receives back in another." (P. 566.)

NB

"Nothing can pass into the ownership of individuals except individual means of consumption." "But, as far as the distribution of the latter among the individual producers is concerned, the same principle prevails as in the exchange of commodity-equivalents, so much labour in one form is exchanged for an equal amount of labour in another form." (P. 567.) This equality of right presupposes *inequality*, inequality in fact, inequality between people, because one is strong, another weak, and so forth (individuals "would not be different individuals if they were not unequal"—p. 567)—one will receive more than another.

Thus:
I. "prolonged birth pangs."
II. "the first phase of communist society."
III. "a higher phase of communist society."

"But these defects are inevitable in the **first phase** of communist society as it is when it has just emerged after prolonged birth pangs from capitalist society. Right can never be higher than the economic structure of society and the cultural development thereby determined."

NB

NB

"In a *higher phase of communist* society, after the enslaving subordination of individuals under division of labour, and therewith also the antithesis between mental and physical labour, has vanished; after labour, from a mere means of life, has itself become the prime necessity of life; after the productive **forces** have also increased with the all-round development of the individual, and all the springs of co-operative wealth flow more abundantly—only then can the **narrow** horizon of **bourgeois right** be fully left behind and society inscribe on its banners: from each according to his ability, to each according to his needs!" (P. 567.)

Thus, here two phases of communist society are clearly, precisely and exactly distinguished:

*The lower* (the "first")—distribution of articles of consumption "proportionately" to the quantity of labour contributed by each to society. Inequality of distribution still considerable. "The narrow bourgeois horizon of rights" *still not fully* passed beyond. This **NB**!! With (semi-bourgeois) rights, it is clear, the (semi-bourgeois) state also has still not fully disappeared. This *Nota Bene*!!

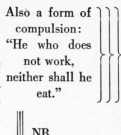

Also a form of compulsion: "He who does not work, neither shall he eat."

NB

*The "higher"*—"from each according to his ability, to each according to his needs." When is this possible? When (1) the antagonism between mental and physical labour has disappeared; (2) labour has become the *prime necessity of life* (NB: the habit of working has become the rule, without compulsion! !); (3) the productive forces have grown considerably, etc. It is clear that the *complete* withering away of the state is possible only at this higher stage. This NB.

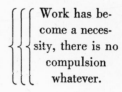

Work has become a necessity, there is no compulsion whatever.

## ENGELS' LETTER OF 1875

In Engels' letter to Bebel of 18-28. III. 1875 there is also a particularly instructive passage, throwing a clearer light than usual on certain sides of Marxism:

(1)   "... In the first place, Lassalle's high-sounding but historically false phrase is accepted (in the Gotha Programme): in contrast to the working class all other classes are only *one reactionary* mass.

NB

(as in
Switzer-
land)

*This statement is only true in a few
exceptional cases;* for instance, *in a* proletarian *revolution like the Commune,* **or** in *a
country* where *not only have* state and society
*been moulded* by the bourgeoisie *in its own
image but where in its wake* the *democratic*
petty bourgeoisie *too has already carried
out* this re-casting *down to its final consequences."* (P. 319.) (But in Germany you have
gone hand in hand with the People's Party
"for years," and you have 7 political de-

NB

mands, "of which there is not a single one
that is not *bourgeois-* [Engels' italics] democratic.")

(2) "...Fifthly, there is not a word
about the organisation of the working class
as a class by means of the *trade unions.* And
that is a very essential point, for *this is the
real class organisation of the proletariat,* in

Exactly!

which it carries on its daily struggles with
capital, in which it trains itself, and which
nowadays even amid the worst reaction
(as in Paris at present) can simply no

NB

longer be smashed. Considering the importance which this form of organisation has also
attained in Germany, it would be absolutely
necessary in our opinion to mention it in the
programme and if possible to leave open a
place for it in the party organisation."
(P. 321.)

(3) "...Equally lacking (in the programme) is the first condition of all freedom:

B

that all functionaries should be responsible
for all their official actions to every citizen
before the ordinary courts and according to
common law." (P. 321.)

(4) "... 'The removal of all social and political inequality' is also a very questionable
phrase in place of 'the abolition of all class
differences.' Between one country and another, one province and another and even one
place and another there will always exist a
*certain inequality* in the conditions of life,
which can be reduced to a minimum but
never entirely removed. Mountain dwellers
will always have different conditions of life
from those of people living on plains. The
idea of socialist society as the realm of
*equality* is a one-sided French idea resting
upon the old 'liberty, equality, fraternity'—an
idea which was justified as a *stage of development* in its own time and place, but which,
like all the one-sided ideas of the earlier
socialist schools, should now be overcome,
for they only produce confusion in people's
heads and more precise modes of presentation
have been found." (P. 322.)

NB

(5) Bakunin, in his work *Statehood and
Anarchy,* makes *us* responsible for every
"thoughtless word" of Liebknecht's.... (Pp.
322-23.)

"thoughtless
word" of
Liebknecht's

(6) "As a rule, *the official programme of
a party is less important than what it does.*
But a *new* programme is after all a banner
publicly raised, and the outside world judges
the party from it." (P. 323) ...

Bebel replied to Engels on 21. IX. 1875,
saying among other things:—"*I am in complete agreement with the judgment* which you
pass on the draft programme, as my letters
to Bracke also prove. (Pp. 334-35.) I also
severely reproached Liebknecht for his readi-

NB
Ha-ha!

ness to give way..." but now that it has been done, "the whole thing is a question of education."

---

That Bebel *himself* not long before shared all these confused views on the subject of the "People's State" is proved by his pamphlet "Our Aims" (9th edition, *1886*, in the "Social-Democratic Library," reprinted without alterations from the 3rd edition of 1872), p. 14: "Thus, the state must be transformed from a state based on *class domination* into a *people's state*... and in this state associated production must take the place of private enterprises"... and here actually, on page 44, he recommends *both* Marx *and* Lassalle! ! ! Side by side! ! At that time Bebel did *not* see the differences between them with regard to the state.

---

## MARX: "THE POVERTY OF PHILOSOPHY"

The passage in **The Poverty of Philosophy** (p. 182) to which Engels refers in his letter of 18-28. III. 1875 (see above)—is evidently the following:

NB "The working class, in the course of its development, will substitute for the old bourgeois society * an association which will exclude classes and their antagonism, and there will be no more political power properly so called, since political power is precisely the official expression of antagonisms in bourgeois society." (*The Poverty of Philosophy*, p. 182, Stuttgart, 1885.) (Preface dated *15. VI. 1847.*)

* In the French original *société civile."—Ed.*

## "THE COMMUNIST MANIFESTO" ON THE STATE *

In *The Communist Manifesto* (XI. 1847) this idea is expressed as follows:

"In depicting the most general phases of the development of the proletariat, we traced the more or less veiled civil war, raging within existing society, up to the point where that war breaks out into open revolution, and where the violent overthrow of the bourgeoisie lays the foundation for the sway of the proletariat." (End of section I.)

And at the end of section II, p. 37, we read:

"We have seen above, that the first step in the revolution by the working class, *is to raise the proletariat to the position of ruling class, to win the battle of democracy.*

"The proletariat will use its political supremacy to wrest, by degrees, all capital from the bourgeoisie, to centralise all instruments of production in *the hands of the state, i.e., of the proletariat organised as the ruling class;* and to increase the total of productive forces as rapidly as possible.

"Of course, in the beginning, this cannot be effected except by means of **despotic inroads** on the rights of property, and on the conditions of bourgeois production; by means of measures, therefore, which appear economically insufficient and untenable, but which, in the course of the movement, outstrip themselves... and are unavoidable as a means of entirely revolutionising the mode of production."...

NB: *The Communist Manifesto:* "The state, *i.e.,* the proletariat organised as the ruling class."

"The state," *i.e.,* the proletariat organised as the ruling class

NB: "despotic inroads"

* All quotations from *The Communist Manifesto* are taken from the authorised English translation (International Publishers, 1932).—*Ed.*

And after enumerating "measures" (§§ 1-10)\* the authors continue:

"the public
power will
lose its
political
character"

"When, in the course of development, class distinctions have disappeared, and all production has been concentrated in the hands of a vast association of the whole nation, the public power will lose its political character. Political power, properly so called, is merely the organised power of one class for oppressing another. If the proletariat during its contest with the bourgeoisie is compelled, by the force of circumstances, to organise itself as a class; if, by means of a revolution, it makes itself the ruling class, and, as such, sweeps away by force the old conditions of production, then it will, along with these conditions, have swept away the conditions for the existence of class antagonisms and of classes generally, and will thereby have abolished its own supremacy as a class."... "The executive of the modern state is but a committee for managing the common affairs of the whole bourgeoisie."

*The Communist Manifesto* speaks of "revolution by the working class," "communist revolution," "proletarian revolution." Seemingly, the term "dictatorship of the proletariat" does not appear as yet. But it is evident that the transformation of the pro-

\* In these measures (§§ 1, 5, 6) the word "state" is used throughout without qualification—for example, § 6: "Centralisation of the means of communication and transport in the hands of the state."

letariat into the "ruling class," its "organisation as the ruling class," its "despotic
inroads on the rights of property," etc., this
*is* "the dictatorship of the proletariat...."

*"The state, i.e., the proletariat organised
as the ruling class*—this is the dictatorship
of the proletariat."    NB

# APPENDIX III

EXTRACTS FROM LENIN'S *THE STATE AND REVOLUTION*

(AUGUST-SEPTEMBER 1917)

CHAPTER IV. SUPPLEMENTARY EXPLANATIONS BY ENGELS

### 3. LETTER TO BEBEL

One of the most remarkable, if not the most remarkable observation on the state in the works of Marx and Engels is contained in the following passage in Engels' letter to Bebel dated March 18-28, 1875. This letter, we may observe in passing, was, as far as we know, first published by Bebel in Volume II of his memoirs (*Aus meinem Leben*), which appeared in 1911, *i.e.*, thirty-six years after it had been written and mailed.

Engels wrote to Bebel criticising the very draft of the Gotha Programme which Marx also criticised in his famous letter to Bracke. Referring particularly to the question of the state, Engels said:

...The free people's state is transformed into the free state. Taken in its grammatical sense a free state is one where the state is free in relation to its citizens and is therefore a state with a despotic government. The whole talk about the state should be dropped, especially since the Commune, which was no longer a state in the proper sense of the word. The *"people's state"* has been thrown in our faces by the anarchists too long, although Marx's book against Proudhon and later *The Communist Manifesto* directly declare that with the introduction of the socialist order of society the state will of itself dissolve [*sich auflöst*] and disappear. As, therefore, the "state" is only a transitory institution which is used in the struggle, in the revolution, in order to hold down [*niederzuhalten*] one's adversaries by force, it is pure nonsense to talk of a "free people's state"; so long as the proletariat still *uses* the state, it does not use it in the interests of freedom but in order to hold down its adversaries, and as soon as it becomes possible to speak of freedom, the state as such ceases to exist. We would therefore propose to replace the word

67

*"state"* everywhere by the word *Gemeinwesen* [community], a good old German word, which can very well represent the French word *"commune."*

It must be borne in mind that this letter refers to the party programme which Marx criticised in a letter dated only a few weeks later than the above (Marx's letter is dated May 5, 1875), and that at the time Engels was living with Marx in London. Consequently, when he says "we" in the last sentence, Engels undoubtedly, in his own as well as in Marx's name, suggests to the leader of the German Workers' Party that the word "state" *be struck out of the programme* and replaced by the word "community."

What a howl about "anarchism" would be raised by the leaders of present-day "Marxism," which has been faked for the convenience of the opportunists, if such a rectification of the programme were suggested to them!

Let them howl. The bourgeoisie will praise them for it.

But we shall go on with our work. In revising the programme of our Party we must unfailingly take the advice of Engels and Marx into consideration in order to come nearer the truth, to restore Marxism, by purging it of distortions, to guide the struggle of the working class for its emancipation more correctly. Certainly no Bolshevik will be found who opposes the advice of Engels and Marx. The only difficulty that may, perhaps, arise will be in regard to terminology. In German there are two words meaning "community," * of which Engels used the one which does *not* denote a single community, but the totality, the system of communities. In Russian there is no such word, and perhaps we may have to decide to use the French word "commune," although this also has its drawbacks.

"The Commune, which was no longer a state in the proper sense of the word"—this is Engels' most important theoretical statement. After what has been said above, this statement is perfectly clear. The Commune *ceased* to be a state in so far as it had to repress, not the majority of the population, but the minority (the ex-

* *Gemeinde* and *Gemeinwesen.—Ed.*

ploiters); it had smashed the bourgeois state machine; in place of a *special* repressive force, the whole population itself came on the scene. All this is a departure from the state in the proper sense of the word. And had the Commune lasted, all traces of the state in it would have "withered away" of themselves; it would not have been necessary for it to "abolish" the institutions of the state; they would have ceased to function in proportion as they ceased to have anything to do.

"The 'people's state' has been thrown in our faces by the anarchists." In saying this, Engels had Bakunin and his attacks on the German Social-Democrats particularly in mind. Engels admitted that these attacks were justified *in so far* as the "people's state" was as much an absurdity and as much a departure from socialism as the "free people's state." Engels tried to put the struggle of the German Social-Democrats against the anarchists on right lines, to make this struggle correct in principle, to purge it of opportunist prejudices concerning the "state." Alas! Engels' letter was pigeonholed for thirty-six years. We shall see below that, even after Engels' letter was published, Kautsky obstinately repeated what in essence were the very mistakes against which Engels had uttered his warning.

Bebel replied to Engels in a letter, dated September 21, 1875, in which he wrote, *inter alia*, that he "fully agrees" with Engels' criticism of the draft programme, and that he had reproached Liebknecht for his readiness to make concessions (p. 304 of the German edition of Bebel's *Memoirs*, Vol. II). But if we take Bebel's pamphlet, *Unsere Ziele*, we find there arguments on the state that are absolutely wrong.

The state must be transformed from one based on *class rule* into a *people's state*. (*Unsere Ziele* [*Our Goal*], German edition, 1886, p. 14.)

This is printed in the *ninth* (the ninth!) edition of Bebel's pamphlet. It is not surprising that such persistently repeated opportunist views on the state were absorbed by German Social-Democracy, especially as Engels' revolutionary interpretations were safely pigeonholed, and all the conditions of everyday life were such as to "wean" the people from revolution for a long time!

CHAPTER V. THE ECONOMIC BASIS OF THE WITHERING AWAY OF
THE STATE

Marx explains this question most thoroughly in his *Critique of the Gotha Programme* (letter to Bracke, May 5, 1875, which was not printed until 1891 in *Neue Zeit*, Vol. IX, 1, and which has appeared in a special Russian edition). The polemical part of this remarkable work, consisting of a criticism of Lassalleanism, has, so to speak, overshadowed its positive part, namely, the analysis of the connection between the development of communism and the withering away of the state.

### 1. Marx's Presentation of the Question

From a superficial comparison of Marx's letter to Bracke (May 5, 1875) with Engels' letter to Bebel (March 28, 1875), which we examined above, it might appear that Marx was much more "pro-state" than Engels, and that the difference of opinion between the two writers on the question of the state was very considerable.

Engels suggested to Bebel that all the chatter about the state be dropped; that the word "state" be eliminated from the programme and the word "community" substituted for it. Engels even declared that the Commune was really no longer a state in the proper sense of the word, yet Marx spoke of the "future state in communist society," *i.e.*, apparently he recognised the need for a state even under communism.

But such a view would be fundamentally wrong. A closer examination shows that Marx's and Engels' views on the state and its withering away were completely identical, and that Marx's expression quoted above refers merely to this *withering away* of the state.

Clearly, there can be no question of defining the exact moment of the *future* "withering away"—the more so since it must obviously be a rather lengthy process. The apparent difference between Marx and Engels is due to the different subjects they dealt with, the different aims they were pursuing. Engels set out to show Bebel plainly, sharply and in broad outline the absurdity of the prevailing prejudices concerning the state, which were shared to no small degree by Lassalle. Marx only touched upon *this* question in passing, being interested in another subject, *viz.*, the *development* of communist society.

The whole theory of Marx is an application of the theory of development—in its most consistent, complete, thought-out and replete form—to modern capitalism. Naturally, Marx was faced with the question of applying this theory both to the *forthcoming* collapse of capitalism and to the *future* development of *future* communism.

On the basis of what *data* can the question of the future development of future communism be raised?

On the basis of the fact that *it has its origin* in capitalism, that it develops historically from capitalism, that it is the result of the action of a social force to which capitalism *has given birth*. There is no trace of an attempt on Marx's part to conjure up a utopia, to make idle guesses about what cannot be known. Marx treats the question of communism in the same way as a naturalist would treat the question of the development of, say, a new biological species, if he knew that such and such was its origin, and such and such the direction in which it was changing.

Marx, first of all, brushes aside the confusion the Gotha Programme brings into the question of the relation between state and society. He writes:

"Present-day society" is capitalist society, which exists in all civilised countries, more or less free from mediæval admixture, more or less modified by the special historical development of each country and more or less developed. On the other hand, the "present-day state" changes with a country's frontier. It is different in the Prusso-German Empire from what it is in Switzerland, it is different in England from what it is in the United States. "*The* present-day state" is therefore a fiction.

Nevertheless, the different states of the different civilised countries, in spite of their manifold diversity of form, all have this in common, that they are based on modern bourgeois society, only one more or less capitalistically developed. They have, therefore, also certain essential features in common. In this sense it is possible to speak of the "present-day state," in contrast to the future in which its present root, bourgeois society, will have died away.

The question then arises: what transformation will the state undergo in

communist society? In other words, what social functions will remain in existence there that are analogous to the present functions of the state? This
question can only be answered scientifically and one does not get a flea-hop
nearer to the problem by a thousand-fold combination of the word people with
the word state.

Having thus ridiculed all talk about a "people's state," Marx
formulates the question and warns us, as it were, that to arrive at
a scientific answer one must rely only on firmly established scientific data.

The first fact that has been established with complete exactitude
by the whole theory of development, by science as a whole—a fact
which the utopians forgot, and which is forgotten by present-day
opportunists who are afraid of the socialist revolution—is that,
historically, there must undoubtedly be a special stage or a special
phase of *transition* from capitalism to communism.

## 2. THE TRANSITION FROM CAPITALISM TO COMMUNISM

Marx continues:

Between capitalist and communist society lies the period of the revolutionary
transformation of the one into the other. There corresponds to this also a
political transition period in which the state can be nothing but *the revolutionary dictatorship of the proletariat.*

Marx bases this conclusion on an analysis of the role played by
the proletariat in modern capitalist society, on the data concerning
the development of this society, and on the irreconcilability of the
antagonistic interests of the proletariat and the bourgeoisie.

Earlier the question was put in this way: in order to achieve its
emancipation, the proletariat must overthrow the bourgeoisie, con-
quer political power and establish its revolutionary dictatorship.

Now the question is put somewhat differently: the transition from
capitalist society—which is developing towards communism—to a
communist society is impossible without a "political transition
period," and the state in this period can only be the revolutionary
dictatorship of the proletariat.

What, then, is the relation of this dictatorship to democracy?
We have seen that *The Communist Manifesto* simply places the
two ideas side by side: "to raise the proletariat to the position of
the ruling class" and "to win the battle of democracy." On the
basis of all that has been said above, it is possible to determine
more precisely how democracy changes in the transition from capitalism to communism.

In capitalist society, under the conditions most favourable to
its development, we have more or less complete democracy in the
democratic republic. But this democracy is always restricted by
the narrow framework of capitalist exploitation, and consequently
always remains, in reality, a democracy for the minority, only for
the possessing classes, only for the rich. Freedom in capitalist society
always remains about the same as it was in the ancient Greek
republics: freedom for the slave-owners. Owing to the conditions
of capitalist exploitation the modern wage-slaves are so crushed by
want and poverty that "they cannot be bothered with democracy,"
"they cannot be bothered with politics"; in the ordinary peaceful
course of events the majority of the population is debarred from
participating in social and political life.

The correctness of this statement is perhaps most clearly proved
by Germany, precisely because in that country constitutional legality
lasted and remained stable for a remarkably long time—for nearly
half a century (1871-1914)—and Social-Democracy during this
period was able to achieve far more in Germany than in other
countries in the way of "utilising legality," and was able to organise
a larger proportion of the working class into a political party than
anywhere else in the world.

What is this largest proportion of politically conscious and active
wage-slaves that has so far been observed in capitalist society? One
million members of the Social-Democratic Party—out of fifteen
million wage-workers! Three million organised in trade unions—
out of fifteen million!

Democracy for an insignificant minority, democracy for the rich
—that is the democracy of capitalist society. If we look more closely
into the mechanism of capitalist democracy, everywhere, in the

"petty"—so-called petty—details of the suffrage (residential qualification, exclusion of women, etc.), in the technique of the representative institutions, in the actual obstacles to the right of assembly
(public buildings are not for "beggars"!), in the purely capitalist
organisation of the daily press, etc., etc.—on all sides we see restriction after restriction upon democracy. These restrictions, exceptions, exclusions, obstacles for the poor, seem slight, especially in
the eyes of one who has never known want himself and has never
been in close contact with the oppressed classes in their mass life
(and nine-tenths, if not ninety-nine hundredths, of the bourgeois
publicists and politicians are of this category); but in their sum
total these restrictions exclude and squeeze out the poor from politics, from taking an active part in democracy.

Marx grasped this *essence* of capitalist democracy splendidly,
when, in analysing the experience of the Commune, he said that
the oppressed are allowed once every few years to decide which
particular representatives of the oppressing class should represent
and suppress them in parliament!

But from this capitalist democracy—inevitably narrow, tacitly
repelling the poor, and therefore hypocritical and false to the core
—forward development does not proceed simply, smoothly and
directly to "greater and greater democracy," as the liberal professors and petty-bourgeois opportunists would have us believe. No,
forward development, *i.e.*, towards communism, proceeds through
the dictatorship of the proletariat, and cannot do otherwise, for the
*resistance* of the capitalist exploiters cannot be *broken* by anyone
else or in any other way.

But the dictatorship of the proletariat, *i.e.*, the organisation of
the vanguard of the oppressed as the ruling class for the purpose
of crushing the oppressors, cannot result merely in an expansion
of democracy. *Simultaneously* with an immense expansion of democracy, which *for the first time* becomes democracy for the poor,
democracy for the people, and not democracy for the rich, the
dictatorship of the proletariat imposes a series of restrictions on
the freedom of the oppressors, the exploiters, the capitalists. We

must crush them in order to free humanity from wage-slavery; their resistance must be broken by force; it is clear that where there is suppression, where there is coercion, there is no freedom, no democracy.

Engels expressed this splendidly in his letter to Bebel when he said, as the reader will remember, that

so long as the proletariat still *uses* the state, it does not use it in the interests of freedom but in order to hold down its adversaries, and as soon as it becomes possible to speak of freedom, the state as such ceases to exist.

Democracy for the vast majority of the people, and suppression by force, *i.e.*, exclusion from democracy, of the exploiters and oppressors of the people—this is the change democracy undergoes during the *transition* from capitalism to communism.

Only in communist society, when the resistance of the capitalists has been completely broken, when the capitalists have disappeared, when there are no classes (*i.e.*, when there is no difference between the members of society as regards their relation to the social means of production), *only then* "the state...ceases to exist," and it *"becomes possible to speak of freedom."* Only then will really complete democracy, democracy without any exceptions, be possible and be realised. And only then will democracy begin to *wither away* owing to the simple fact that, freed from capitalist slavery, from the untold horrors, savagery, absurdities and infamies of capitalist exploitation, people will gradually *become accustomed* to observing the elementary rules of social intercourse that have been known for centuries and repeated for thousands of years in all copy-book maxims; they will become accustomed to observing them without force, without compulsion, without subordination, *without the special apparatus* for compulsion which is called the state.

The expression "the state *withers away"* is very well chosen, for it indicates both the gradual and the spontaneous nature of the process. Only habit can, and undoubtedly will, have such an effect; for we see around us millions of times how readily people become accustomed to observing the necessary rules of social intercourse if there is no exploitation, if there is nothing that causes indignation, that calls forth protest and revolt or evokes the necessity for *suppression*.

Thus, in capitalist society we have a democracy that is curtailed, wretched, false; a democracy only for the rich, for the minority. The dictatorship of the proletariat, the period of transition to communism, will for the first time create democracy for the people, for the majority, in addition to the necessary suppression of the minority—the exploiters. Communism alone is capable of giving really complete democracy, and the more complete it is the more quickly will it become unnecessary and wither away of itself.

In other words: under capitalism we have a state in the proper sense of the word, that is, a special machine for the suppression of one class by another, and of the majority by the minority at that. Naturally, the successful discharge of such a task as the systematic suppression of the exploited majority by the exploiting minority calls for the greatest ferocity and savagery in the work of suppression, it calls for seas of blood through which mankind has to wade in slavery, serfdom and wage-labour.

Furthermore, during the *transition* from capitalism to communism, suppression is *still* necessary; but it is now the suppression of the exploiting minority by the exploited majority. A special apparatus, a special machine for suppression, the "state," is *still* necessary, but this is now a transitory state; it is no longer a state in the proper sense; for the suppression of the minority of exploiters by the majority of the wage-slaves of *yesterday* is comparatively so easy, simple and natural a task that it will entail far less bloodshed than the suppression of the risings of slaves, serfs or wage-labourers, and it will cost mankind far less. This is compatible with the extension of democracy to such an overwhelming majority of the population that the need for a *special machine* of suppression will begin to disappear. The exploiters are, naturally, unable to suppress the people without a very complex machine for performing this task; but *the people* can suppress the exploiters even with a very simple "machine," almost without a "machine," without a special apparatus, by the simple *organisation of the armed masses* (such as the Soviets of Workers' and Soldiers' Deputies, we may remark, running ahead a little).

Finally, only communism makes the state absolutely unnecessary, for there is *no one* to be suppressed—"no one" in the sense of a *class*, in the sense of a systematic struggle against a definite section of the population. We are not utopians, and we do not in the least deny the possibility and inevitability of excesses on the part of *individual persons* or the need to suppress *such* excesses. But, in the first place, no special machine, no special apparatus of repression is needed for this; this will be done by the armed people itself, as simply and as readily as any crowd of civilised people, even in modern society, parts two people who are fighting, or interferes to prevent a woman from being assaulted. And, secondly, we know that the fundamental social cause of excesses, which consist in violating the rules of social intercourse, is the exploitation of the masses, their want and their poverty. With the removal of this chief cause, excesses will inevitably begin to *"wither away."* We do not know how quickly and in what order, but we know that they will wither away. With their withering away, the state will also *wither away.*

Without indulging in utopias, Marx defined more fully what can be defined *now* regarding this future, namely, the difference between the lower and higher phases (degrees, stages) of communist society.

## 3. THE FIRST PHASE OF COMMUNIST SOCIETY

In the *Critique of the Gotha Programme*, Marx goes into some detail to disprove Lassalle's idea that under socialism the worker will receive the "undiminished" or "whole proceeds of his labour." Marx shows that from the whole of the social labour of society it is necessary to deduct a reserve fund, a fund for the expansion of production, for the replacement of "used up" machinery, and so on; then, also, from the means of consumption must be deducted a fund for the costs of administration, for schools, hospitals, homes for the aged, and so on.

Instead of Lassalle's hazy, obscure, general phrase ("the whole proceeds of his labour for the worker") Marx makes a sober estimate of exactly how socialist society will have to manage its affairs. Marx proceeds to make a *concrete* analysis of the conditions of life of a society in which there will be no capitalism, and says:

What we have to deal with here [in analysing the programme of the workers' party] is a communist society, not as it has *developed* on its own foundations, but, on the contrary, as it *emerges* from capitalist society; which is thus in every respect, economically, morally and intellectually, still stamped with the birthmarks of the old society from whose womb it emerges.

And it is this communist society—a society which has just come into the world out of the womb of capitalism and which, in every respect, bears the birthmarks of the old society—that Marx terms the "first," or lower, phase of communist society.

The means of production are no longer the private property of individuals. The means of production belong to the whole of society. Every member of society, performing a certain part of socially-necessary labour, receives a certificate from society to the effect that he has done such and such an amount of work. And with this certificate, he draws from the social stock of means of consumption, a corresponding quantity of products. After deduction of the amount of labour which goes to the public fund, every worker, therefore, receives from society as much as he has given it.

"Equal right" apparently reigns supreme.

But when Lassalle, having such a social order in view (usually called socialism, but termed by Marx the first phase of communism), speaks of this as "equitable distribution," and says that this is "the equal right" of "all members of society" to "equal proceeds of labour," he is mistaken, and Marx exposes his error.

"Equal right," says Marx, we indeed have here; but it is *still* a "bourgeois right," which, like every right, *presupposes inequality*. Every right is an application of an *equal* standard to *different* people who, in fact, are not alike and are not equal to one another; that is why "equal right" is really a violation of equality and an injustice. As a matter of fact, every man, having performed as much social labour as another, receives an equal share of the social product (after the above-mentioned deductions).

But people are not alike: one is strong, another is weak; one is married, another is not; one has more children, another has less, and so on. And the conclusion Marx draws is:

... with an equal output, and hence an equal share in the social consumption fund, one will in fact receive more than another, one will be richer than another, and so on. To avoid all these defects, right, instead of being equal, would have to be unequal.

Hence, the first phase of communism cannot yet produce justice and equality; differences, and unjust differences, in wealth will still exist, but the *exploitation* of man by man will have become impossible, because it will be impossible to seize the *means of production*, the factories, machines, land, etc., as private property. In smashing Lassalle's petty-bourgeois, confused phrases about "equality" and "justice" *in general,* Marx shows the *course of development* of communist society, which, at first, is *compelled* to abolish *only* the "injustice" of the means of production having been seized by private individuals, and which *cannot* at once abolish the other injustice of the distribution of articles of consumption "according to the amount of labour performed" (and not according to needs).

The vulgar economists, including the bourgeois professors and also "our" Tugan-Baranovsky, constantly reproach the Socialists with forgetting the inequality of people and with "dreaming" of abolishing this inequality. Such a reproach, as we see, only proves the extreme ignorance of Messieurs the bourgeois ideologists.

Marx not only scrupulously takes into account the inevitable inequality of men, but he also takes into account the fact that the mere conversion of the means of production into the common property of the whole of society (usually called "socialism") *does not remove* the defects of distribution and the inequality of "bourgeois right" which *continue to prevail* as long as products are divided "according to the amount of labour performed." Continuing, Marx says:

But these defects are inevitable in the first phase of communist society as it is when it has just emerged after prolonged birth pangs from capitalist society. Right can never be higher than the economic structure of society and the cultural development thereby determined.

And so, in the first phase of communist society (usually called socialism) "bourgeois right" is *not* abolished in its entirety, but only in part, only in proportion to the economic transformation so far attained, *i.e.*, only in respect of the means of production. "Bourgeois right" recognises them as the private property of individuals. Socialism converts them into *common* property. *To that extent*— and to that extent alone—"bourgeois right" disappears.

However, it continues to exist as far as its other part is concerned; it continues to exist in the capacity of regulator (determining factor) in the distribution of products and the allotment of labour among the members of society. The socialist principle: "He who does not work, neither shall he eat," is *already* realised; the other socialist principle: "An equal amount of labour for an equal amount of products," is also *already* realised. But this is not yet communism, and it does not yet abolish "bourgeois right," which gives to unequal individuals, in return for an unequal (actually unequal) amount of labour, an equal amount of products.

This is a "defect," says Marx, but it is unavoidable in the first phase of communism; for if we are not to indulge in utopianism, we must not think that having overthrown capitalism people will at once learn to work for society *without any standard of right;* and indeed, the abolition of capitalism *does not immediately* create the economic premises for *such* a change.

And there is as yet no other standard than that of "bourgeois right." To this extent, therefore, there is still need for a state, which, while safeguarding the public ownership of the means of production, would safeguard equality of labour and equality in the distribution of products.

The state withers away in so far as there are no longer any capitalists, any classes, and, consequently, no *class* can be *suppressed.*

But the state has not yet completely withered away, since there still remains the safeguard of "bourgeois right" which sanctifies actual inequality. For the complete withering away of the state, complete communism is necessary.

## 4. THE HIGHER PHASE OF COMMUNIST SOCIETY

Marx continues:

> In a higher phase of communist society, after the enslaving subordination of individuals under division of labour, and therewith also the antithesis between mental and physical labour, has vanished; after labour, from a mere means of life, has itself become the prime necessity of life; after the productive forces have also increased with the all-round development of the individual, and all the springs of co-operative wealth flow more abundantly—only then can the narrow horizon of bourgeois right be fully left behind and society inscribe on its banners: from each according to his ability, to each according to his needs!

Only now can we appreciate to the full the correctness of Engels' remarks in which he mercilessly ridiculed the absurdity of combining the words "freedom" and "state." While the state exists there is no freedom. When there will be freedom, there will be no state.

The economic basis for the complete withering away of the state is such a high stage of development of communism that the antithesis between mental and physical labour disappears, that is to say, when one of the principal sources of modern *social* inequality disappears —a source, moreover, which cannot be removed immediately by the mere conversion of the means of production into public property, by the mere expropriation of the capitalists.

This expropriation will *facilitate* the enormous development of the productive forces. And seeing how capitalism is already *retarding* this development to an incredible degree, seeing how much progress could be achieved even on the basis of the present level of modern technique, we are entitled to say with the fullest confidence that the expropriation of the capitalists will inevitably result in the enormous development of the productive forces of human society. But how rapidly this development will proceed, how soon it will reach the point of breaking away from the division of labour, of removing the antithesis between mental and physical labour, of transforming labour into "the prime necessity of life"—we do not and *cannot* know.

That is why we have a right to speak only of the inevitable withering away of the state, emphasising the protracted nature of this process and its dependence upon the rapidity of development of the *higher phase* of communism, and leaving the question of length of time, or the concrete forms of the withering away, quite open, because there is *no* material for an answer to these questions.

The state will be able to wither away completely when society applies the rule: "From each according to his ability, to each according to his needs," *i.e.*, when people have become so accustomed to observing the fundamental rules of social intercourse and when their labour is so productive that they will voluntarily work *according to their ability*. "The narrow horizon of bourgeois right," which compels one to calculate with the stringency of a Shylock whether he has not worked half an hour more than another, whether he is not getting less pay than another—this narrow horizon will then be left behind. There will then be no need for society to regulate the quantity of products to be distributed to each; each will take freely "according to his needs."

From the bourgeois point of view, it is easy to declare that such a social order is "a pure utopia," and to sneer at the Socialists for promising everyone the right to receive from society, without any control of the labour of the individual citizen, any quantity of truffles, automobiles, pianos, etc. Even now, most bourgeois "savants" confine themselves to sneering in this way, thereby displaying at once their ignorance and their mercenary defence of capitalism.

Ignorance—for it has never entered the head of any Socialist to "promise" that the higher phase of the development of communism will arrive; and the great Socialists, in *foreseeing* its arrival, presuppose not the present productivity of labour *and not the present* ordinary run of people, who, like the seminary students in Pomyalovsky's story,* are capable of damaging the stocks

* Pomyalovsky's *Seminary Sketches* depicted a group of student-ruffians who engaged in destroying things for the pleasure it gave them.—*Ed.*

of social wealth "just for fun," and of demanding the impossible.

Until the "higher" phase of communism arrives, the Socialists demand the *strictest* control, by society *and by the state*, of the measure of labour and the measure of consumption; but this control must *start* with the expropriation of the capitalists, with the establishment of workers' control over the capitalists, and must be carried out, not by a state of bureaucrats, but by a state of *armed workers*.

The mercenary defence of capitalism by the bourgeois ideologists (and their hangers-on like Messrs. Tsereteli, Chernov and Co.) lies in their *substituting* controversies and discussions about the distant future for the essential and imperative questions of *present-day* policy, *viz.*, the expropriation of the capitalists, the conversion of *all* citizens into workers and employees of *one* huge "syndicate"— the whole state—and the complete subordination of the whole of the work of this syndicate to the really democratic *state of the Soviets of Workers' and Soldiers' Deputies*.

In reality, when a learned professor, and following him some philistine, and following him Messrs. Tsereteli and Chernov talk of the unreasonable utopias, of the demagogic promises of the Bolsheviks, of the impossibility of "introducing" socialism, it is the higher stage or phase of communism they have in mind, which no one has ever promised, or even thought to "introduce," because, generally speaking, it cannot be "introduced."

And this brings us to the question of the scientific difference between socialism and communism which Engels touched on in his above-quoted argument about the incorrectness of the name "Social-Democrat." The political difference between the first, or lower, and the higher phase of communism will in time, probably, be tremendous; but it would be ridiculous to take cognisance of this difference now, under capitalism; and only isolated anarchists, perhaps, could invest it with primary importance (if there are still any people among the anarchists who have learned nothing from the "Plekhanovist" conversion of the Kropotkins, the Graveses, the Cornelisens and other "leading lights" of anarchism into social-chauvinists or "anarcho-trenchists," as Ge, one of the few anarchists who has still preserved a sense of honour and a conscience, has expressed it).

But the scientific difference between socialism and communism is clear. What is usually called socialism was termed by Marx the "first" or lower phase of communist society. In so far as the means of production become *common* property, the word "communism" is also applicable here, providing we do not forget that it is *not* complete communism. The great significance of Marx's explanations is that here, too, he consistently applies materialist dialectics, the doctrine of development, and regards communism as something which develops *out* of capitalism. Instead of scholastically invented, "concocted" definitions and fruitless disputes about words (what is socialism? what is communism?), Marx gives an analysis of what may be called the stages in the economic ripeness of communism.

In its first phase, or first stage, communism *cannot* as yet be fully ripe economically and entirely free from traditions and traces of capitalism. Hence the interesting phenomenon that communism in its first phase retains "the narrow horizon of *bourgeois* right." Of course, bourgeois right in regard to distribution of articles of *consumption* inevitably presupposes the existence of the *bourgeois state*, for right is nothing without an apparatus capable of *enforcing* the observance of the standards of right.

Consequently, not only bourgeois right, but even the bourgeois state for a certain time remains under communism, without the bourgeoisie!

This may sound like a paradox or simply a dialectical puzzle, of which Marxism is often accused by people who do not take the slightest trouble to study its extraordinarily profound content.

But as a matter of fact, remnants of the old surviving in the new confront us in life at every step, both in nature and in society. And Marx did not arbitrarily insert a scrap of "bourgeois" right into communism, but indicated what is economically and politically inevitable in a society emerging *from the womb* of capitalism.

Democracy is of great importance to the working class in its struggle for emancipation from the capitalist. But democracy is by no means a boundary that must not be overstepped; it is only one of the stages on the road from feudalism to capitalism, and from capitalism to communism.

Democracy means equality. The great significance of the proletariat's struggle for equality, and the significance of equality as a slogan will be clear if we correctly interpret it as meaning the abolition of *classes*. But democracy means only *formal* equality. As soon as equality is obtained for all members of society *in relation to* the ownership of the means of production, that is, equality of labour and equality of wages, humanity will inevitably be confronted with the question of going beyond formal equality to real equality, *i.e.*, to applying the rule, "from each according to his ability, to each according to his needs." By what stages, by what practical measures humanity will proceed to this higher aim—we do not and cannot know. But it is important to realise how infinitely mendacious is the ordinary bourgeois conception of socialism as something lifeless, petrified, fixed once for all, whereas in reality *only* under socialism will a rapid, genuine, really mass forward movement, embracing first the *majority* and then the whole of the population, commence in all spheres of social and personal life.

Democracy is a form of state, one of its varieties. Consequently, it, like every state, on the one hand represents the organised, systematic application of force against persons; but, on the other hand, it signifies the formal recognition of the equality of all citizens, the equal right of all to determine the structure and administration of the state. This, in turn, is connected with the fact that, at a certain stage in the development of democracy, it first rallies the proletariat as the revolutionary class against capitalism, and enables it to crush, smash to atoms, wipe off the face of the earth the bourgeois, even the republican bourgeois, state machine, the standing army, the police and bureaucracy and to substitute for them a *more* democratic state machine, but a state machine nevertheless, in the shape of the armed masses of workers who are being transformed into a universal people's militia.

Here "quantity is transformed into quality": *such* a degree of democracy implies overstepping the boundaries of bourgeois society, the beginning of its socialist reconstruction. If, indeed, *all* take part in the administration of the state, capitalism cannot retain its hold. And the development of capitalism, in turn, itself creates the *premises* that really *enable* "all" to take part in the administration of the state. Some of these premises are: universal literacy, which is already achieved in a number of the most advanced capitalist countries, then the "training and disciplining" of millions of workers by the huge, complex, socialised apparatus of the post-office, the railways, the big factories, large-scale commerce, banking, etc., etc.

Given these *economic* premises it is quite possible, after the overthrow of the capitalists and bureaucrats, to proceed immediately, overnight, to supersede them in the *control* of production and distribution, in the work of *keeping account* of labour and products by the armed workers, by the whole of the armed population. (The question of control and accounting must not be confused with the question of the scientifically trained staff of engineers, agronomists and so on. These gentlemen are working today and obey the capitalists; they will work even better tomorrow and obey the armed workers.)

Accounting and control—that is the *main* thing required for the "setting up" and correct functioning of the *first phase* of communist society. *All* citizens are transformed into the salaried employees of the state, which consists of the armed workers. *All* citizens become employees and workers of a *single* national state "syndicate." All that is required is that they should work equally—do their proper share of work—and get paid equally. The accounting and control necessary for this have been *simplified* by capitalism to an extreme and reduced to the extraordinarily simple operations —which any literate person can perform—of checking and recording, knowledge of the four rules of arithmetic, and issuing receipts.*

---

* When most of the functions of the state are reduced to this accounting and control by the workers themselves, it will cease to be a "political state," and the "public functions will lose their political character and be transformed into simple administrative functions" (*cf.* above, chapter IV, § 2, on Engels' controversy with the anarchists [not included in these excerpts; see *State and Revolution*, Little Lenin Library, Vol. 14.—*Ed.*]).

When the *majority* of the people begin independently and everywhere to keep such accounts and maintain such control over the capitalists (now converted into employees) and over the intellectual gentry who preserve their capitalist habits, this control will really become universal, general, national; and there will be no way of getting away from it, there will be "nowhere to go."

The whole of society will have become a single office and a single factory with equality of labour and equality of pay.

But this "factory" discipline, which the proletariat will extend to the whole of society after the defeat of the capitalists and the overthrow of the exploiters, is by no means our ideal, or our ultimate goal. It is but a necessary *step* for the purpose of thoroughly purging society of all the hideousness and foulness of capitalist exploitation, and *for further* progress.

From the moment all members of society, or even only the vast majority, have learned to administer the state *themselves*, have taken this business into their own hands, have "set up" control over the insignificant minority of capitalists, over the gentry who wish to preserve their capitalist habits, and over the workers who have been profoundly corrupted by capitalism—from this moment the need for government begins to disappear altogether. The more complete democracy, the nearer the moment approaches when it becomes unnecessary. The more democratic the "state" which consists of the armed workers and which is "no longer a state in the proper sense of the word," the more rapidly does *the state* begin to wither away altogether.

For when *all* have learned to administer, and actually do administer social production independently, independently keep accounts and exercise control over the idlers, the gentlefolk, the swindlers and similar "guardians of capitalist traditions," the escape from this national accounting and control will inevitably become so incredibly difficult, such a rare exception, and will probably be accompanied by such swift and severe punishment (for the armed workers are practical men and not sentimental intellectuals, and they will scarcely allow anyone to trifle with them), that very soon the *necessity* of observing the simple, fundamental rules of human intercourse will become a *habit*.

And then the door will be wide open for the transition from the first phase of communist society to its higher phase, and with it to the complete withering away of the state.

# APPENDIX IV

## PROGRAMME OF THE GERMAN WORKERS' PARTY [115]

### DRAFT

## I.

1. Labour is the source of all wealth and all culture and since useful labour is only possible in society and through society, the proceeds of labour belong undiminished with equal right to all members of society.[116]

2. In present-day society, the instruments of labour are the monopoly of the capitalist class; the resulting dependence of the working class is the cause of misery and servitude in all its forms.

3. The emancipation of labour demands the promotion of the instruments of labour to the common property of society, and the co-operative regulation of the total labour with equitable distribution of the proceeds of labour.[117]

4. The emancipation of labour must be the work of the working class, in contrast to which all other classes are only one reactionary mass.

5. The working class strives for its emancipation first of all within the framework of the present-day national state, conscious that the necessary result of its efforts, which are common to the workers of all civilised countries, will be the international brotherhood of peoples.[118]

## II.

Starting from these basic principles, the German Workers' Party strives by all legal means for the free state and socialist society; the abolition of the wage system together with the iron law of wages and exploitation in every form; the removal of all social and political inequality.[119]

### III.

The German Workers' Party, in order to pave the way to the solution of the social question, demands the establishment of producers' co-operative societies with state aid under the democratic control of the toiling people. The producers' co-operative societies are to be called into being for industry and agriculture in such dimensions that the socialist organisation of the total labour will arise from them.

### IV.[120]

A. The German Workers' Party demands as the free basis of the state:

1. Universal, equal, direct and secret suffrage for all males of twenty-one years and above, for all elections—national and local.

2. Direct legislation by the people with right of initiating proposals and veto.

3. Universal conscription. People's militia in place of the standing army. Decision on war and peace through the people's representatives.

4. Abolition of all exceptional laws, especially the laws on the press, association and assembly.

5. Administration of justice by the people. Free administration of justice.

B. The German Workers' Party demands as the intellectual and moral basis of the state: [121]

1. Universal and equal elementary education through the state. Universal compulsory school attendance. Free instruction.

2. Freedom of science. Freedom of conscience.[122]

C. The German Workers' Party demands as the economic basis of the state: [123]

A single progressive income tax for state and local administration, in place of all existing, and especially indirect, taxes.

D. The German Workers' Party demands for the protection of

the working class against the power of capital within present-day society: [124]

1. Freedom of association.

2. Normal working day [125] and prohibition of Sunday labour.

3. Restriction of women's labour and prohibition of child labour.[126]

4. State supervision of factory, workshop and domestic industry.[127]

5. Regulation of prison labour.

6. An effective liability law.

# EXPLANATORY NOTES

1. Compare *Capital*, Vol. I, pp. 197-98 (Kerr edition): "Labour is, in the first place, a process in which both man and nature participate, and in which man of his own accord starts, regulates, and controls the material reactions between himself and nature. He opposes himself to nature as one of her own forces, setting in motion arms and legs, head and hands, the natural forces of his body, in order to appropriate nature's productions in a form adapted to his own wants. By thus acting on the external world and changing it, he at the same time changes his own nature."

2. Compare the following passage in *Capital*, Vol. II, p. 44: "Whatever the social forms of production may be, workers and means of production always remain the factors of it.... For production to take place at all they must unite. The special manner in which this union is accomplished distinguishes the different economic epochs from one another."

3. Jean-Jacques Rousseau (1712-78); French philosopher and publicist of the period of the Enlightenment. As a petty-bourgeois ideologist, Rousseau was the theoretician of consistent bourgeois democracy. He was a passionate champion of the struggle against feudal exploitation and absolutism, and defended the theory of the "sovereignty of the people." He based his criticism of the feudal system on an abstract, unhistorical theory of natural equality, of a primitive happy communist condition of humanity, and of the superiority of nature and inborn qualities over culture. In his *Marginal Notes*, Marx points out that the Gotha Programme, instead of giving a scientific class analysis of the social order and of the law of its development, confines itself to the repetition of an abstract preaching which recalls that of Rousseau.

4. Ferdinand Lassalle (1825-64); German politician and publicist who played a big role in the history of the German workers' movement. In the beginning of the 'sixties, when the workers' movement was developing throughout Germany, Lassalle founded the General Association of German Workers, thus bringing into being the first mass political organisation of German workers independent of the bourgeois-democratic parties. In this lies his historical importance. At one time under Marx's influence, and in touch with Marx both by personal contact and by letter, Lassalle called himself a "pupil" of Marx; but he did not adopt the standpoint of the proletarian revolution. He directed the party which he had brought into being along an opportunist path, he put forward reformist slogans and advocated the path to socialism through a "free," *i.e.*, bourgeois, state with universal suffrage and through producers' co-

operative societies enjoying the aid of the Prussian government. In the political question of foremost importance at that time, *viz.*, the question of the unification of Germany, which it was possible to solve either by revolution or by dynastic wars waged by Prussia, Lassalle played directly into the hands of the Prussian *Junker* government, by entering into an understanding with Bismarck. "Lassalle and the Lassalleans," Lenin wrote in 1913, "seeing that the chances of the proletarian and democratic way to unity were weak, pursued vacillating tactics adapted to the hegemony of the *Junker*, Bismarck. Their errors led to the deviation of the workers' party along the path of Bonapartist state socialism." ("August Bebel," 1913, *Collected Works*, Russian ed., Vol. XVI, p. 547.) "Lassalle," Lenin wrote in 1915, "was ... during his flirting with Bismarck ... an opportunist. Lassalle was adapting himself to the victory of Prussia and Bismarck, to the absence of sufficient strength on the part of the democratic national movements of Italy and Germany. Thus, Lassalle deviated in the direction of a national liberal-labour policy, whereas Marx encouraged and developed an independent, consistently democratic policy hostile to national-liberal cowardice. (Prussia's interference in the War of 1859 against Napoleon would have stimulated the national movement in Germany.) Lassalle cast glances not down, but up, fascinated by Bismarck. Bismarck's success by no means justified Lassalle's opportunism." ("Under a Stolen Flag," *Collected Works*, Vol. XVIII, International Publishers, New York, p. 122.) Throughout the whole history of the German working class movement Lassalleanism was the inspiration of the opportunists. During the war, and after it, the social-chauvinists and opportunists frequently put forward—and still put forward—the slogan: "Back to Lassalle!"

5. The reference is to the Statutes of the International Workingmen's Association (First International), which were written by Marx in November 1864. (See note 23.) The corresponding point in the Statutes runs: "The economical subjection of the man of labour to the monopoliser of the means of labour, that is the sources of life, lies at the bottom of servitude in all its forms, of all social misery, mental degradation and political dependence."

6. Marx refers to Lassalle's "contract" with Bismarck, the existence of which was suspected by Marx and Engels. Their suspicions were only confirmed after the death of Lassalle. In his letter to Kugelmann, February 23, 1865, Marx writes:

"However, it soon became clear—the proofs fell into our hands—that *Lassalle* had in fact *betrayed* the party. He had entered into a formal contract with Bismarck (of course, *without having any sort of guarantees in his hand*). At the end of September 1864 he was to go to Hamburg and there ... *force* Bismarck to annex Schleswig-Holstein, that is, he was to proclaim its incorporation in the name of the 'workers,' etc. In return for this Bismarck promised universal suffrage and a few socialist charlatanries. It is a pity that Lassalle could not play the comedy through to the end. The hoax would have made him look damned ridiculous and foolish, and would have put a stop forever to all attempts of that sort."

Marx did not know (it was only brought to light in 1928) that Lassalle had concluded his contract with Bismarck not shortly before his death but considerably earlier, in the beginning of May 1863. Consequently he had conducted negotiations with Bismarck even *before* the foundation of the General Association of German Workers; one can even assume that the association was founded by secret agreement with Bismarck. For a characterisation of "Royal Prussian Socialism" one may quote here a passage of Lassalle's letter of June 8, 1863, to Bismarck: "The working class is...inclined...to see in the crown the natural bearer of social dictatorship, in opposition to the egoism of bourgeois society, if the crown for its part...could make up its mind ...to pursue a really revolutionary and national trend and to transform itself from a monarchy of the privileged estates into a social and revolutionary people's monarchy." (Gustav Mayer, *Bismarck und Lassalle. Ihr Briefwechsel und ihre Gespräche* [*Bismarck and Lassalle. Their Correspondence and Conversations*], Berlin, 1928, page 60.)

7. In *Capital*, Marx calls the total value of the product "the value of the product," while he calls the new part of the value added to it by labour "the new value" or "the newly produced value." (Compare *Capital*, Vol. I, chap. VIII, "Constant Capital and Variable Capital"; chap. IX, sec. 2, "The Representation of the Components of the Value of the Product by Corresponding Proportional Parts of the Product Itself"; chap. IX, sec. 3, "Senior's 'Last Hour.'" In connection with "new value," see also chap. XVII, "Changes of Magnitude in the Price of Labour Power and in Surplus Value.")

8. In 1872 Marx wrote about sectarian socialism in his pamphlet directed against the Bakuninists (*Les prétendues scissions dans l'Internationale* [*The Alleged Splits in the International*]): "The first phase in the struggle of the proletariat against the bourgeoisie is marked by the sectarian movement. This is justifiable at a time when the proletariat is not yet sufficiently developed to act as a class. Isolated thinkers subject the social antagonisms to criticism and at the same time give a fantastic solution of them which the mass of the workers have only to accept as complete, to propagate and to put into practical operation. It is in the nature of these sects, which are founded on the initiative of individuals, that they keep themselves aloof and remote from every real activity, from politics, strikes, trade unions, in a word, from every collective movement. The mass of the proletariat always remains indifferent, even hostile, to their propaganda. The workers of Paris and Lyons were as little interested in the Saint-Simonists, Fourierists and Icarians, as the English Chartists and trade unionists in the Owenites. The sects, at the outset a lever for the movement, become an obstacle as soon as this movement has overtaken them; they

then become reactionary. The proof of this is the sects in France and England and recently the Lassalleans in Germany, who, after having for years hindered the organisation of the proletariat, have finally become simple police tools. In short, they represented the infancy of the proletarian movement just as astrology and alchemy represented the infancy of science."

9. In his pamphlet *The Housing Question*, Engels also criticises the "socialist" demand for the "whole proceeds of labour," attacking the system of the French petty-bourgeois socialist Proudhon (see note 62), who also advocated this demand. He writes: "It is, moreover, self-evident that, with social production conditioned by modern large-scale industry [that is, under communism], it is possible to assure each person 'the whole proceeds of his labour,' so far as this phrase has any meaning at all. And it has a meaning only if it is extended to mean not that each individual worker becomes the possessor of 'the whole proceeds of his labour,' but that the whole of society, consisting entirely of workers, becomes the possessor of the total proceeds of its labour, which it partly distributes among its members for consumption, partly uses for replacing and increasing the means of production and partly stores up as a reserve fund for production and consumption." (*The Housing Question*, International Publishers, New York, p. 31.)

10. Compare with this refutation of Lassalle's demand for the "undiminished" or "whole proceeds of Labour," Lenin, *The State and Revolution*, chap. V, sec. 3: "The First Phase of Communist Society" (pp. 77-81 of this book).

11. In *Anti-Dühring* (chap. X) Engels writes as follows in regard to the demand for equality:

"The demand for equality in the mouth of the proletariat has therefore a double meaning. It is either—as was especially the case at the very start, for example in the Peasants' War—the spontaneous reaction against the crying social inequalities, against the contrast of rich and poor, the feudal lords and their serfs, surfeit and starvation; as such it is the simple expression of the revolutionary instinct, and finds its justification in that, and indeed only in that. Or, on the other hand, the proletarian demand for equality has arisen as the reaction against the bourgeois demand for equality, drawing more or less correct and more far-reaching demands from this bourgeois demand, and serving as an agitational means in order to rouse the workers against the capitalists on the basis of the capitalists' own assertions; and in this case it stands and falls with bourgeois equality itself. In both cases the real content of the proletarian demand for equality is the demand for the *abolition of classes*. Any demand for equality which goes beyond that, of necessity passes into absurdity." (*Herr Dühring's Revolution in Science* [*Anti-Dühring*], International Publishers, New York, p. 123.)

In his work *Economics and Politics in the Period of the Proletarian Dictatorship*, Lenin writes in connection with Engels' statement:

"Long ago Engels in his *Anti-Dühring* explained that the conception of equality is a cast from the relations of commodity production and becomes transformed into a prejudice if equality is not understood to mean the *abolition of classes*. This elementary truth regarding the distinction between the bourgeois-democratic and the socialist conceptions of equality is constantly being forgotten. But if it is not forgotten, it becomes obvious that by overthrowing the bourgeoisie the proletariat takes a decisive step towards the abolition of classes, and that in order to complete the process the proletariat must continue its class struggle, making use of the apparatus of state power and of all methods of combating, influencing and bringing pressure to bear on the overthrown bourgeoisie and the vacillating petty bourgeoisie." (*Selected Works,* Vol. VIII, International Publishers, New York, p. 13.) Compare the passages in *The State and Revolution* (see pp. 78, 79, 80 and 85 of this book), in which Lenin in part quotes, in part summarises and develops the ideas put forward by Marx in the *Critique*.

12. See Lenin's elucidation on pp. 79-80 of this book.

13. See Lenin's elucidation on pp. 81-82 of this book. In connection with Communist *subbotniks* (volunteer labour groups) Lenin said in December 1919: "If we were to ask ourselves in what way communism differs from socialism, we would have to reply that socialism is the society which grows directly out of capitalism, that it is the first form of the new society. Communism, on the other hand, is a higher form of society, which can develop only when socialism has taken firm hold. Socialism implies the performance of work without the aid of capitalists, it implies social labour accompanied by the strictest accounting, control and supervision on the part of the organised vanguard, the most advanced section of the toilers. Moreover, it implies that standards of labour and the amount of compensation for labour must be determined. They must be determined because capitalist society has left us such relics and habits as uncoordinated labour, lack of confidence in social economy, the old habits of the small producer, which prevail in all peasant countries. All these run counter to a real communist economy. Communism, on the other hand, is the name we apply to a system under which people become accustomed to the performance of public duties without any specific machinery of compulsion, when unpaid work for the common good becomes the general phenomenon." (*Selected Works,* Vol. VIII, p. 239.) Compare also Lenin's article "From the Destruction of the Ancient Social System to the Creation of the New," *Selected Works,* Vol. IX, p. 446.

14. In *Capital,* Vol. II, p. 133 (Kerr edition), Marx says: "It is, moreover, in accordance with the bourgeois horizon, which is entirely bounded by the craze for making money, not to see in the character of the mode of production the basis of the corresponding mode of circulation but *vice versa.*" The question of the relation of production to distribution, exchange and consumption

is analysed by Marx in detail in his unfinished *Introduction to the Critique of Political Economy* (1857), which was published together with his *Contribution to the Critique of Political Economy*. In his article "The Economic Content of Narodism and the Criticism of it in Mr. Struve's Book" (1894), Lenin refers to the passage from the *Critique of the Gotha Programme* as follows: "Marx contrasts vulgar socialism to scientific socialism, which does not attach great importance to distribution, and which explains the social system by the organisation of relations of *production* and which considers that the given system of organisation of relations of production already includes a definite system of distribution. This idea ... runs like a thread through the whole of Marx's teachings." (Lenin, *Selected Works*, Vol. I, p. 460.)

15. Literally, the preamble to the Provisional Rules of the Association begins as follows: "Considering, that the emancipation of the working classes must be conquered by the working classes themselves...."

16. In Greek tragedies the chorus consisted of a strophe and an antistrophe.

17. See the criticism of this thesis made by Engels in his letter to Bebel of March 18, 1875 (p. 28). Marx and Engels in criticising this slogan constantly pointed out the significance of the allies of the proletariat in all stages of the class struggle of the proletariat. On this subject, Engels wrote to Bernstein on November 2, 1882: "The real weakness is the childish notion of the coming revolution which is supposed to *begin* by 'Guelfs here, Ghibellines there,' the whole world dividing itself into two armies: we here, the 'one reactionary mass' there. That means that the revolution is to begin with the *fifth act*, and not with the first in which the mass of all the oppositional parties stands together against the government and its blunders and thus is victorious, upon which the separate parties among the victors one after another wear themselves out, make themselves impossible, until finally by this means the mass of the people is thrust wholly onto our side and then Vollmar's much-vaunted decisive battle can proceed." Lenin also says: "To imagine that social revolution is *conceivable* without revolts by small nations in the colonies and Europe, without the revolutionary outbursts of a section of the petty bourgeoisie *with all its prejudices,* without a movement of non-class-conscious proletarian and semi-proletarian masses against the oppression of the landlords, the church, the monarchy, the foreign nations, etc.—to imagine that means *repudiating social revolution.* Apparently they imagine that in one place an army will line up and say, 'We are for socialism,' and in another place another army will say, 'We are for imperialism,' and that this will be social revolution! ... Whoever expects a 'pure' social revolution will *never* live to see it. Such a person pays lip service to revolution, without understanding what revolution is. The Russian Revolution of 1905 was a bourgeois-democratic revolution. It consisted of a series of battles in which all the discontented classes, groups and elements of the population participated.... *Objectively,* the mass movement broke the back of tsarism and paved

the way for democracy; and for that reason the class-conscious workers led it. The socialist revolution in Europe *cannot be anything else* than an outburst of mass struggle on the part of all and sundry of the oppressed and discontented elements." ("Discussion on Self-Determination Summed Up," *Selected Works,* Vol. V, pp. 303-4.)

18. See Karl Marx and Frederick Engels, *The Communist Manifesto,* International Publishers, 1932, p. 19.

19. The paragraph of the *Manifesto* from which this is taken runs:

"The lower middle class, the small manufacturer, the shopkeeper, the artisan, the peasant, all these fight against the bourgeoisie, to save from extinction their existence as fractions of the middle class. They are therefore not revolutionary, but conservative. Nay more, they are reactionary, for they try to roll back the wheel of history. If by chance they are revolutionary, they are so only in view of their impending transfer into the proletariat; they thus defend not their present, but their future interests; they desert their own standpoint to adopt that of the proletariat." (*Ibid.,* p. 19.)

20. The elections to the Reichstag here referred to took place in January 1874.

21. See note 6.

22. Marat (1743-93); one of the most outstanding revolutionary leaders of the French bourgeois revolution at the end of the eighteenth century, a Jacobin. By "the Marat of Berlin," Marx ironically refers to Hasselmann, the chief editor of the *Neuer Sozialdemokrat,* the central organ of the Lassalleans.

23. The First International, the International Workingmen's Association (1864-72), under Marx's guidance "laid the foundation of the international organisation of the working class for preparing their revolutionary assault on capital." (Lenin, *Collected Works,* Russian ed., Vol. XXIV, p. 247.) In his essay, "Karl Marx," Lenin summarises its history as follows:

"The period of revival of the democratic movements at the end of the 'fifties and the 'sixties recalled Marx to practical activity. In 1864 (September 28) the International Workingmen's Association—the famous First International—was founded in London. Marx was the heart and soul of this organisation; he was the author of its first Address and of a host of resolutions, declarations and manifestoes. By uniting the labour movement of various countries, by striving to direct into the channel of joint activity the various forms of non-proletarian, pre-Marxian socialism (Mazzini, Proudhon, Bakunin, liberal trade unionism in England, Lassallean vacillations to the Right in Germany, etc.), and by combating the theories of all these sects and schools, Marx hammered out a uniform tactic for the proletarian struggle of the working class in the various countries. After the fall of the Paris Commune (1871) ... and after the International was split by the Bakuninists, the existence of that organisation in Europe became impossible. After the Hague Congress of the International (1872) Marx had the General Council of the International transferred to New York. The First International had accomplished its historical role and it made way for a period of immeasurably larger growth of the labour movement in all the countries of the world, a period, in fact, when the movement grew in *breadth* and when *mass* socialist labour parties in individual national states were created." (See "The Teachings of Karl Marx," *Little Lenin Library*, Vol. I, International Publishers.) The introduction to the *Programme of the Communist International* contains the following: "As the united and centralised international party of the proletariat, the Communist International is the only party to continue the principles of the First International, and to carry them out upon the new mass foundation of the revolutionary proletarian movement."

24. The passages in the *Manifesto* run: "Though not in substance, yet in form, the struggle of the proletariat with the bourgeoisie is at first a national struggle. The proletariat of each country must, of course, first of all settle matters with its own bourgeoisie." (P. 20.) And again: "The workingmen have no country. We cannot take from them what they have not got. Since the proletariat must first of all acquire political supremacy, must rise to be the leading class of the nation, must constitute itself *the* nation, it is, so far, itself national, though not in the bourgeois sense of the word." (P. 28.)

25. In 1890 Engels described Bismarck's *international* policy as follows: "The War of 1859 had also alarmed Prussia. Prussia almost doubled its army, and put at the helm a man who at least on one point could compete with Russian diplomacy—in his lack of scruple as to the means used. This man was Bismarck. During the Polish rising in 1863—as opposed to Austria, France and England—he theatrically took his stand with Russia and did all he could to help Russia to victory. This secured for him the tsar's abandonment of his usual policy in the Schleswig-Holstein question; in 1864, with the tsar's consent, the Duchy was torn from Denmark. Then came the Austro-Prussian War; and once again the tsar rejoiced at the second drubbing of Austria and the growth of the power of Prussia—his only loyal vassal—loyal even after the kicks of 1849-50. The War of 1866 brought in its train the Franco-Prussian War of 1870, and once again the tsar sided with his Prussian *dyadya molodyets* [good old uncle]; he held a direct threat over Austria and thus deprived France of the only ally who could have saved her from complete defeat. But Alexander in 1870, like Louis Bonaparte in 1866, was cheated by the quick successes of the German arms." ("The Foreign Policy of Russian Tsarism," *Neue Zeit*, 1890, pp. 198-99.) With regard to the significance of the Franco-Prussian War, the most outstanding success of Bismarck's foreign policy, Lenin wrote in *Socialism and War:* "In the Franco-Prussian War, Germany robbed France, but this does not change the fundamental historical significance of that war, as having freed tens of millions of the German people from feudal de-

centralisation and from the oppression of two despots, the Russian tsar and Napoleon III." (*Collected Works*, Vol. XVIII.)

26. The International League of Peace and Freedom was an international organisation of bourgeois democrats and pacifist free traders which existed in the 'sixties and 'seventies. The First International, at the insistence of Marx and under his leadership, carried on a decisive struggle against this League which was founded in Geneva in 1867. The watchwords of the League were "Universal Brotherhood of Peoples" and "The United States of Europe." (See Engels' reference to this League on p. 29.)

27. After the fall of the Paris Commune, Bismarck attempted in 1871-72 to conclude a formal treaty between Germany, Austria and Russia for the purpose of united persecution of the revolutionary movement in general and the First International in particular. Although a formal treaty was not arrived at, the government organs of the big Powers, nevertheless, were already then taking joint action against the revolutionaries.

28. The *Norddeutsche Allgemeine Zeitung*, Bismarck's organ, published, on March 20, 1875 (No. 67), a leading article on the draft programme of the Social-Democratic Party. Special attention was drawn to point five of the programme which Marx is referring to here, and in connection with this point the comment was made that the Social-Democrats apparently "desire to free themselves to a certain extent from the influence of the International," that "the Social-Democratic agitation has in many respects become more prudent," and that "it is renouncing the International."

29. Engels, who shared Marx's opinion of the "internationalism" of the Gotha Programme, wrote to F. Becker on August 13, 1875: "In Germany... since the fusion with the Lassalleans, the connection with the International—which was in any case a loose one—has been entirely broken off."

30. Lassalle formulated this "law" as follows: "The iron economic law which, under present-day conditions, under the rule of the supply and demand of labour, determines wages is this: that the average wage always remains reduced to the necessary basis of subsistence that...is requisite for existence and propagation." (*An Open Answer to the Central Committee for Convening a General Congress of German Workers at Leipzig*, Zurich, 1863.) See also the criticism of this law in Engels' letter to Bebel of March 18-28, 1875 (p. 30).

31. F. A. Lange (1828-75); a German Neo-Kantian philosopher, petty-bourgeois democratic writer, author of a work on social reform, *The Labour Question: Its Significance for the Present and the Future* (first published in 1865). In his letter to Kugelmann of June 27, 1870, Marx says: "Herr Lange (*Ueber die Arbeiterfrage*, etc., second edition) sings my praises loudly, but with the object of making himself important. Herr Lange, you see, has made a great discovery. The whole of history can be brought under a single great natural law. The natural law is the *phrase* (in this application Darwin's ex-

pression becomes nothing but a phrase) 'struggle for life,' and the content of this phrase is the Malthusian law of population or, rather, overpopulation. So instead of analysing the struggle for life as represented historically in varying and definite forms of society, all that has to be done is to translate every concrete struggle into the phrase, 'struggle for life,' and this phrase itself into the Malthusian population fantasy. One must admit that this is a very impressive method—for swaggering, sham-scientific, bombastic ignorance and intellectual laziness." (*Letters to Dr. Kugelmann*, International Publishers, p. 111.) With regard to the Malthusian "law," see the following note.

32. Thomas Robert Malthus (1766-1834) ; English economist. In his work, *An Essay on the Principle of Population* (1798), he developed the idea that there exists an immutable law of population according to which the population increases in geometrical progression while the means of subsistence necessary for its maintenance increase only in arithmetical progression. Consequently, according to Malthus, the basis for poverty lies in the natural contradiction between the rapid increase in the population and the restricted increase of the necessary means of subsistence. Marx, who called Malthus' work a libel on the human race, pointed out the falsity of this "law" and proved that "in fact every special historic mode of production has its own special laws of population, historically valid within its limits alone." (*Capital*, Vol. I, chap. XXIII, Section 3. *Ibid.*, Sections 2 and 3, see the criticism of Malthus' theory and the exposition of the law of population peculiar to the capitalist mode of production.)

33. Lassalle was killed in a duel in September 1864.

34. In *The Condition of the Working Class in England in 1844*, Engels wrote of capitalist wage slavery as follows:

"The worker is, in law and in fact, the slave of the property-holding class, of the bourgeoisie, so effectually a slave that he is sold like a piece of goods, rises and falls in price like a commodity. If the demand for workers increases, the price of workers rises; if it falls, their price falls. If it falls so greatly that a number of them become unsalable, if they are 'left in stock,' they are simply left idle; and as they cannot live upon that, they die of starvation.... The only difference as compared with the old outspoken slavery is this, that the worker of today *seems* to be free because he is not sold once for all, but piecemeal, by the day, the week, the year, and because no one owner sells him to another, but he is forced to sell himself in this way instead, being the slave of no particular person, but of the whole property-holding class. For him the matter is unchanged at bottom, and if this semblance of freedom necessarily gives him some *real* freedom on the one hand, it entails on the other the disadvantage that no one guarantees him a subsistence, that he is in danger of being repudiated at any moment by his master, the bourgeoisie, and left to die of starvation, if the bourgeoisie ceases to have an interest in his employment, his existence. The bourgeoisie, on the other hand, is far better off under the present arrangement than under the old slave system; it can dismiss its employees at discretion without sacrificing invested capital, and gets its work done much more cheaply than is possible with slave labour, as Adam Smith comfortably pointed out."

35. Buchez (1796-1865); French historian and writer. In the 'forties of the last century, he was the representative of French Catholic "socialism," which demanded the formation of producers' co-operative societies with state aid as a means of struggle against the growing revolutionary movement. See Engels' letter to Bebel of March 18-28, 1875, p. 27 of this edition.

36. Louis Philippe (1773-1850); King of France in the period of the "July Monarchy." The July Revolution of 1830 put him on the throne and the February Revolution of 1848 brought his reign to an end.

37. *Atelier* (*Workshop*); a monthly journal published in Paris (1840-48). Its contributors, editors and publishers were all workers. The *Atelier* group was under the influence of the reactionary Catholic socialism of Buchez. In politics it supported the bourgeois radicals.

38. In regard to this thesis, Lenin wrote in the autumn of 1916: "Up to now this axiom has never been disputed by socialists, and yet it implies the recognition of the *state* right up to the time when victorious socialism will have grown into complete communism." ("Discussion on Self-Determination Summed Up," *Collected Works*, Russian ed., Vol. XIX.) This formulation already contains the essence of the entire fifth chapter of *The State and Revolution*, which is included as an appendix to this edition. In 1922, the renegade Kautsky "corrected" this thesis of Marx in the following way: "In the interval between the purely bourgeois administration and the purely proletarian administration of a democratic state there is the period of transition from one to the other. To this also corresponds a political transition period, when the government as a rule, takes the form of a coalition government." (K. Kautsky, *The Proletarian Revolution and its Programme*, Stuttgart, 1922.)

39. See Lenin's note on this passage of the *Critique*, p. 53.

40. The German People's Party or Democratic Party was founded in September 1865 in Darmstadt and reorganised at the Stuttgart Party Congress in September 1868. It was the party of the petty bourgeoisie of oppositional and partly also revolutionary inclination in the smaller and medium-sized states of Germany, and particularly of South Germany. In opposition to Bismarck's policy of the unity of Germany under the hegemony of monarchist *Junker* Prussia, it put forward the establishment of a democratic German republic. It was closely connected with the International League of Peace and Freedom (see note 26) and it made efforts to gain influence among the workers. It assisted in the creation of various workers' educational associations and played the leading role in the annual congresses of the German Workers' Associations. The

organisation of the People's Party in Saxony, which consisted almost exclusively of members of the Workers' Associations, was used by W. Liebknecht and A. Bebel, who carried on agitation within the framework of the People's Party as the basis for the foundation of an independent workers' party. Later, the People's Party rapidly lost its influence over the workers when Liebknecht and Bebel, at the insistence of Marx and Engels, succeeded in securing the adherence of the German Workers' Associations to the First International at their Nuremberg Congress in September 1868. In August 1869 the Social-Democratic Workers' Party was founded at the Eisenach Congress of the Workers' Associations.

41. The reference here is to Napoleon III (Louis Bonaparte), Emperor of France (1851-70).

42. Referring to this characterisation of the constitution of the new Hohenzollern German Empire, Lenin wrote in 1913: "Marx estimated the actual essence of the German 'constitution' a hundred thousand times *more profoundly* than hundreds of professors, priests and publicists of the bourgeoisie, who chanted the praises of the 'state based on law.' They crawled on their bellies before the success and triumph of the highly placed favourites in Germany. Marx estimated the class essence of the policy, being guided not by a particular 'kink' in events, but by the *whole* experience of *international* democracy and of the international workers' movement." (*Collected Works*, Russian ed., Vol. XVII, p. 100.)

43. See Lenin's note on this passage in the *Critique*, on p. 54.

44. The reference is to R. Gladstone (1805-75), a big merchant in Liverpool, a Liberal who propagated the idea of a progressive income tax which should fall primarily on the big landowners. He was the brother of William Gladstone (1809-98), the prominent British Liberal Prime Minister of the last half of the nineteenth century.

45. Lenin wrote: "*Der Kulturkampf*, the 'Struggle for Culture,' *i.e.*, the struggle Bismarck waged in 1870 against the German Catholic Party, the party of the 'Centre,' by means of a police persecution of Catholicism. By this struggle Bismarck only *stimulated* the militant clericalism of the Catholics, and only injured the work of real culture, because he gave prominence to religious divisions rather than political divisions and diverted the attention of certain sections of the working class and of democracy from the urgent tasks of the class and revolutionary struggle to a most superficial and mendacious bourgeois anti-clericalism." ("The Attitude of the Workers' Party Towards Religion," in "Religion," *Little Lenin Library*, vol. 7.)

46. *Ibid.*, p. 70: the Workers' Party "regards religion as a private matter *in relation to the state*, but by no means in relation to itself, to Marxism, or to the Workers' Party."

47. This appendix contains "demands for the protection of the working

class against the power of capital within present-day society." The first point, with which Marx does not deal, demands "freedom of association."

48. "I have spoken and saved my soul," that is to say, I have done my duty.

49. August Bebel (1840-1913); a cabinet-maker by trade; one of the most prominent leaders of the international working class movement in the second half of the nineteenth and beginning of the twentieth century; one of the founders and leaders both of German Social-Democracy and of the Second International. He was active in what Lenin described as "the period of organisation and adolescence of mass socialist parties of a class proletarian composition." Under the strong influence of Marx and Engels, who gave him their support and criticised the theoretical and tactical errors of an opportunist character committed by him, Bebel was able to lay the foundations of a really mass workers' party. After Engels' death in 1895, in the conditions of the imperialist epoch, Bebel was no longer equal to the position of a revolutionary proletarian leader. It is true that he sharply opposed Bernsteinism—open opportunism—but in practice he adapted himself to the opportunism which had grown strong in German Social-Democracy (and in the whole Second International). This Centrism showed itself also in his relations with Bolshevism, in his endeavours, along with Kautsky and others, to water down Bolshevism into Menshevism.

50. Wilhelm Hasenclever, Wilhelm Hasselmann and Wilhelm Tölcke were leaders of the General Association of German Workers. The first named was chairman of the party from 1871 to 1875; after the fusion with the Eisenachers he occupied various important party posts but did not play any leading role; he died in 1889. The second became an anarchist during the period of the Anti-Socialist Law and in 1880 was expelled from the party. Tölcke (1817-93) remained in the ranks of the German Social-Democratic Party until his death, but he played no important part in the leadership of the united party.

51. The programme of the Social-Democratic Workers' Party of Germany, led by W. Liebknecht and A. Bebel, which was founded at the Eisenach Congress in August 1869 (the party of the "Eisenachers"). See note 40.

52. The reference is to the Eisenachers.

53. See Marx's criticism of this Lassallean phrase on pp. 11-12; also note 17.

54. For the People's Party see note 40. The Eisenachers remained even after 1871 in political contact with the Left wing of the People's Party. This Left wing was headed by J. Jacoby, an old democrat and republican hostile to the Bismarckian empire. In this connection, Liebknecht, the leader of the Eisenachers, was not able to distinguish sufficiently sharply and expose the difference in principle between the oppositional policy of petty-bourgeois democracy on the one hand and the revolutionary policy of the proletarian socialist party on the other. Marx and Engels frequently took Liebknecht to task for this Right opportunist mistake that was of advantage to the Lassalleans.

55. The *Volksstaat* [*People's State*] was the central organ of the Eisenachers from 1870 to 1876. It appeared twice weekly in Leipzig; its editor was W. Liebknecht.

56. The *Frankfurter Zeitung* was at that time an oppositional paper, the organ of the South German petty-bourgeois democrats; it adopted a social reform standpoint in regard to the "labour question."

57. See the Draft on pp. 89-91; also Marx's criticism on pp. 18-19.

58. From the very beginning of the Franco-Prussian War of 1870-71 the German Social-Democratic workers, in a number of resolutions and manifestoes, expressed their hostility to the German war-lords and their solidarity with the French workers; after the Prussian victory at Sedan they demanded "a peace that was honourable for France" and protested against the annexation of Alsace-Lorraine. In the Reichstag, Bebel and Liebknecht made a sharp protest against the war, and abstained from voting the war credits; after Sedan, they voted *against* war credits. (Further details are given in the two manifestoes of the General Council of the First International in connection with the Franco-Prussian War; these were written by Marx. See *The Civil War in France*, International Publishers.) In his Prefatory Note written on July 1, 1874, to *The Peasant War in Germany* (International Publishers), Engels wrote: "As early as 1870, the German workers were subjected to a severe test: the Bonapartist war provocation and its natural effect: the general national enthusiasm in Germany. The German socialist workers did not let themselves be led astray for a single moment. Not a trace of national chauvinism showed among them. In the midst of the wildest intoxication of victory they remained cool, demanding 'an equitable peace with the French Republic and no annexations' and not even martial law was able to silence them. No battle glory, no talk of German 'imperial magnificence' produced any effect on them; their sole aim remained the liberation of the entire European proletariat. We may surely say that in no other country up to now have the workers been put to so hard a test and passed through it so brilliantly."

59. Two speeches made by Lassalle in Frankfort-on-the-Main on May 17 and 19, 1863, were published by the General Association of German Workers under the title *Arbeiterlesebuch* (*Workers' Reader*). Engels refers to the passage in the first speech which was taken by Lassalle from his pamphlet *An Open Answer to the Central Committee for Convening a General Congress of German Workers at Leipzig* (Zurich, 1863). The passage is quoted in note 30.

60. Wilhelm Bracke (1843-80); one of the leaders of the Eisenachers. He stood very close to Marx and Engels, and supported them, though not very energetically, in their struggle against the opportunist errors of the Gotha Programme. In 1873 he wrote a pamphlet, *The Lassallean Proposal*. The pamphlet was directed against the tenth point in the Eisenach programme of 1869, dealing with state aid for workers' producers' co-operative societies;

it gives a detailed criticism of the Lassallean movement. In his foreword to this pamphlet, Bracke wrote: "After I had become acquainted with Karl Marx's works and had joined the Eisenach party, I became more and more convinced that an attempt to realise that [Lassalle's] proposal would not only not be useful but would be harmful to the workers' movement...." (See also note 71.)

61. Amand Gögg (1820-97); a petty-bourgeois democrat from Baden. He played an important part in the Revolution of 1848-49; in the 'sixties he conducted pacifist propaganda. He was one of the leaders of the bourgeois League of Peace and Freedom. (See note 26.)

62. Pierre Joseph Proudhon (1808-65); a petty-bourgeois theoretician. In the third, critical chapter of *The Communist Manifesto* Proudhon figures among the "conservative or bourgeois" socialists. "Not to destroy capitalism and its foundation—commodity production, but to *purify* that foundation from abuses, excrescences, etc.; not to destroy exchange and exchange value, but, on the contrary, to 'constitute' it, to make it general, absolute, *'just,'* free from fluctuations, crises, abuses—that is Proudhon's idea." (Lenin, "Critical Notes on the National Question," 1913, *Collected Works*, Russian ed., Vol. XVII, p. 145.) Proudhon recognised the necessity of the organisation of the proletariat, but only in the form of all kinds of co-operative societies, which, so to speak, build socialism behind the back of capitalism. Denying the necessity for the participation of the proletariat in political struggle, Proudhon became the theoretician of peaceful anarchism. Proudhonism, during the period of the First International, had a big influence on the working class movement in a number of Latin countries in whose national economy small production played a predominant role. The struggle of Marx and Engels against Proudhonism in the First International led to the victory of Marxism. Proudhonism has retained a certain influence among the anarcho-syndicalists of France and Spain up to the present time. Marx's book against Proudhon appeared in French in 1847 under the title *Misère de la Philosophie* (*The Poverty of Philosophy*, International Publishers). The passage which Engels has in mind is quoted by Lenin in his notebook *Marxism on the State* (see p. 62 of the present edition).

63. The corresponding place in *The Communist Manifesto* is also quoted by Lenin in the notebook; see p. 64 of the present edition.

64. We quote here a forgotten statement of Engels on the withering away of the state and on the dictatorship of the proletariat from a letter of his to the American Socialist van Patten on April 18, 1883: "Since 1845 Marx and I have held the view that *one* of the ultimate results of the future proletarian revolution will be the gradual dissolution and final disappearance of the political organisation known by the name of *state*. The main object of this organisation has always been to secure, by armed force, the economic oppression

of the labouring majority by the minority which alone possesses wealth. With the disappearance of an exclusively wealth-possessing minority, there also disappears the necessity for the power of armed oppression, or state power. At the same time, however, it was always our view that in order to attain this and the other far more important aims of the future social revolution, the working class must first take possession of the organised political power of the state and by its aid crush the resistance of the capitalist class and organise society anew. This is to be found already in *The Communist Manifesto* of 1847, chapter II, conclusion.

"The anarchists put the thing upside down. They declare that the proletarian revolution must *begin* by doing away with the political organisation of the state. But after its victory the sole organisation that the proletariat finds already in existence is precisely the state. This state may require very considerable alterations before it can fulfil its new functions. But to destroy it at such a moment would be to destroy the only organism by means of which the victorious proletariat can assert its newly conquered power, hold down its capitalist adversaries and carry out the economic revolution of society without which the whole victory must end in a new defeat and in a mass slaughter of the workers similar to those after the Paris Commune." *The Correspondence of Marx and Engels,* International Publishers, pp. 416-17.

65. Lenin attached great fundamental importance to this proposition. (See pp. 48-49 of the present edition.)

66. Why Marx and Engels did not come forward publicly against this opportunist programme after its acceptance is explained in the letter of Engels to Bracke of October 11, 1875. (See pp. 36-38.)

67. The reference is to Bakunin's book, *Statehood and Anarchy. The Struggle of the Two Parties in the International Workingmen's Association* (1873). In this book Bakunin speaks of Liebknecht as "an agent of K. Marx," and makes Marx responsible for all the theoretical and tactical errors made by Liebknecht, who "acts under Marx's direct guidance."

68. Wilhelm Liebknecht (1826-1900); one of the most important figures in the German and international working class movements in the second half of the nineteenth century. He took part in the 1848-49 Revolution as a South-German democrat. In the 'fifties he emigrated to London, where under Marx's influence he became a socialist. In 1868-69, he was the founder, together with Bebel, of the Social-Democratic Workers' Party of Germany (the "Eisenachers") and conducted an energetic agitation for the revolutionary method of achieving German unification—often, however, falling into "Austrophilism" and defending particularism. He carried on a fight against the Lassalleans. During the Franco-Prussian War he took up a revolutionary-internationalist position. For several decades he was chief editor of the party's central organ, a member of the Party Executive, a Reichstag deputy, etc. Liebknecht's agitation influenced

the proletarian masses by his class struggle propaganda, and instilled in them hatred of the capitalist system. In *What Is To Be Done?* (1902) Lenin speaks of him as the model of a "people's tribune." As political leader of the party he committed serious opportunist errors, which had their roots in his non-dialectical mode of thought and his tendency to reverence for vulgar democracy. Liebknecht was primarily responsible for the serious theoretical and tactical errors of the Eisenachers prior to the Gotha unification in 1875, and also for the confusion immediately following on the promulgation of Bismarck's Exceptional Law against the socialists. In the inner-party conflict on the question of voting for the steamship subsidies in 1885 he adopted a conciliatory position. He was often at loggerheads with Bebel, whose attitude—under Engels' guidance—was more correct on a number of questions. Liebknecht, who carried on a fight against the ruling classes and the government, in 1872 himself said that he was "a soldier of the revolution"; but at the same time he often preached the Lassallean idea of a peaceful "cultural" revolution, denying the role of violence in the socialist revolution. Nevertheless, his revolutionary enthusiasm, showing itself in his agitational activity, bound him closely to the revolutionary wing of the working class movement, and at the end of his life Liebknecht was an opponent of opportunists of the type of Millerand, Bernstein, etc. In 1907, in his foreword to the Russian translation of Liebknecht's pamphlet *No Compromises* (1889), Lenin characterised his tactics in the question of agreements with opposition bourgeois parties as a model of revolutionary tactics, contrasting them with the tactics of the Mensheviks. (Lenin, *Collected Works*, Russian ed., Vol. X, pp. 215-20.)

69. *Demokratisches Wochenblatt* [*Democratic Weekly*] was the organ of the Eisenachers prior to their formal separation from the petty-bourgeois radical People's Party of Saxony. It was edited by W. Liebknecht and published in Leipzig in 1868-69.

70. On account of the revolutionary-internationalist position they adopted during the Franco-Prussian War of 1870-71, Liebknecht and Bebel were sentenced in March 1872 in the famous Leipzig trial for state treason to two years' imprisonment in a fortress. Bebel's term of imprisonment ended on May 14, 1874, but six weeks later he was again imprisoned in Zwickau, Saxony, for a further nine months, for *"lèse majesté."* He was finally released on April 1, 1875, which happened to coincide with Bismarck's birthday.

71. Bracke in his letter to Engels of March 25, 1875, sharply criticised the Gotha Programme. He said: "The acceptance of this programme is impossible for me, and Bebel also is of the same opinion as regards himself." Bracke directed his main attack against the point in the programme on the establishment of producers' co-operatives by state aid. In Bracke's opinion, the acceptance of this point turned the party into a sect. He wrote: "Since Bebel appears to be determined to take up the struggle, I should feel myself com-

pelled at least to support him with all my strength. I should, however, like very much to know in advance how you and Marx regard the matter. Your experience is riper, your understanding is better than mine.... If you agree in regard to this, then I will make a proposal to Bebel so that we can come forward to the congress with a common draft programme." Bebel, however, did not justify Bracke's hopes and did not come out against the programme.

72. Ramm; a German Social-Democrat, one of the editors of the Leipzig *Volksstaat*, the central organ of the Eisenach party. He did not play any leading role in the party.

73. Together with this letter Marx sent Bracke his *Critique of the Gotha Programme*. In 1891 Engels published the *Critique* together with this letter.

74. August Geib (1842-79); Treasurer of the Eisenach party, a member of the Reichstag from 1874. Ignaz Auer (1846-1907); Secretary of the Eisenach party, subsequently one of the leaders of the reformist wing of German Social-Democracy.

75. The reference is to Bakunin's work *Statehood and Anarchy*. (See note 67.)

76. The Unity Congress was held on May 22-27, 1875, in Gotha; the congress of the Lassalleans had taken place previously in May and the congress of the Eisenachers was held afterwards in Hamburg on June 8.

77. The first French translation of Volume I of *Capital* was edited by Marx himself, and was published in Paris in separate parts during the years 1872-75.

78. Bernhard Becker (1826-82); German historian and publicist, one of the founders of Lassalle's General Association of German Workers. After Lassalle's death, and in accordance with the testament left by Lassalle, he was elected chairman of the party. Early in 1866 he broke with the Lassalleans and subsequently joined the Eisenachers. (See note 81.)

79. Marx's pamphlet, *Revelations about the Cologne Communist Trial*, was written in 1853; it was republished by the *Volksstaat* Publishing House with a postscript by Marx dated January 8, 1875.

80. In accordance with the new statutes, three governing bodies were elected at the Gotha Congress: the administrative board, the control commission and the committee. The committee's function was to intervene in the event of disagreement between the administrative board and the control commission.

81. The reference is to the committee's proposal to remove from the list of party literature the anti-Lassallean works of B. Becker (*Revelations About the Tragic Death of Ferdinand Lassalle*, Schlietz, 1868; *The History of Lassalle's Working Class Agitation*, Braunschweig, 1874), and W. Bracke's *The Lassallean Proposal* (Braunschweig, 1873). See notes 60 and 78.

82. Leopold Sonnemann (1831-1909); German politician and publicist, one of the leaders of the People's Party, editor of the *Frankfurter Zeitung*. (See

note 56.) In the 'sixties and 'seventies his opposition to Bismarck's policy brought him close to the Eisenachers on a number of questions.

83. Julius Vahlteich (1839-1915); shoemaker by trade, one of the most prominent leaders of the Eisenach party. At one period he was a Lassallean, but he opposed Lassalle's dictatorship and was expelled from the General Association of German Workers.

84. Karl Hirsch (1841-1900); a well-known German socialist journalist, who at that time was close to Marx and Engels.

85. The administrative board consisted of the Lassalleans—Hasenclever, Hartmann and Derossi, and the Eisenachers—Geib and Auer.

86. Wilhelm Stieber was a leading official of the Prussian political police. He was a bitter persecutor of revolutionary proletarian organisations, and used the vilest methods in fabricating evidence against accused persons— falsifying documents, using false evidence, bribery, burglaries, etc. He was in charge of the investigations connected with the Cologne Communist Trial in 1852. His machinations on that occasion were exposed by Marx in his pamphlet *Revelations about the Cologne Communist Trial*, 1853.

87. Tessendorf, public prosecutor in Prussia, acquired fame in the 'sixties and 'seventies as a "specialist in political cases against socialists."

88. The Leipzigers, *i.e.*, Liebknecht and other members of the editorial board of the party's central organ, *Volksstaat*.

89. The first subsequent Reichstag elections took place early in 1877.

90. The last point (No. 10) of the "immediate demands," in the programme of the Social-Democratic Workers' Party (adopted at Eisenach in August 1869), reads as follows: "State aid for co-operatives and state credits for the free producers' co-operative associations, with democratic guarantees."

91. See note 60.

92. Engels refers to Marx's *Critique of the Gotha Programme*. But he was wrong in assuming that Bebel was acquainted with the *Critique*. When the *Critique* was published by Engels in 1891, it came to light that W. Liebknecht, in spite of Marx's express request (see his letter to Bracke on p. 34), had not shown this document to Bebel. "That in May-June 1875," Engels states, "the document was deliberately concealed from Bebel and hidden away soon became clear to me." (Letter to Kautsky, February 11, 1891.) Bebel only saw it in 1891, when the *Critique* was already published in the *Neue Zeit*. It must be added that, having read the *Critique* before the issue appeared, Bebel tried to stop its publication and sent a telegram to this effect, but it was already too late. (See *Vorwärts*, Berlin, February 26, 1891.)

93. See Engels' earlier letter to Bracke, March 11, 1875, and notes 81-84.

94. Engels wrote this foreword to the *Critique* when it was published in 1891 in the *Neue Zeit*. For the history of its publication, see Engels' letter to K. Kautsky, February 23, 1891, in this edition, pp. 42-45.

95. See above, Marx's letter to Bracke, May 5, 1875.

96. The Congress of the German Social-Democratic Party at Halle—the first congress after the abrogation of the Anti-Socialist Law—decided on October 16, 1890, on the motion of W. Liebknecht, the main author of the Gotha Programme, to prepare a draft of a new programme for the next party congress. The resolution drafted by Liebknecht and accepted by the congress gave as the reason for the decision that the Gotha Programme, "however excellently it had justified itself in the battles of the last fifteen years, especially under the Anti-Socialist Law, was nevertheless not up-to-date in all points...." The new programme of German Social-Democracy was adopted at the Erfurt Congress (the "Erfurt programme"). In comparison with the Gotha Programme it was a great step forward, but in spite of Engels' insistent demands it was silent on the question of the dictatorship of the proletariat, and among the transitional demands it did not even contain the demand for a democratic republic.

97. The fifth, Hague Congress of the First International, held in September 1872, was dominated by the struggle between the Bakuninists on the one hand and the General Council, under the leadership of Marx and Engels, on the other. The majority of the congress supported the General Council. Bakunin was expelled. But the Bakuninists continued the fight against the General Council even after the Hague Congress. Two or three years later, the First International—the International Workingmen's Association—formally ceased to exist, after "dominating European history for ten years, in one direction—in the direction towards the future...." (Engels' letter to Sorge, September 12-17, 1874).

98. On the most important theoretical and practical differences between Marxism and Bakuninism, Lenin wrote (in the *Tasks of the Proletariat in our Revolution*) : "The difference between Marxism and anarchism is that Marxism recognises *the necessity of the state* for the purpose of the transition to socialism; but (and here is where we differ from Kautsky and Co.) *not* a state of the type of the usual, parliamentary, bourgeois, democratic republic, but a state like the Paris Commune of 1871 and the Soviets of Workers' Deputies of 1905 and 1917." (Lenin, *Selected Works*, Vol. VI, p. 73.)

"*In those days*, after the defeat of the Paris Commune, history demanded slow organisational and educational work.... The anarchists were then (as they are now) fundamentally wrong not only theoretically, but also economically and politically. The anarchists wrongly estimated the character of the times, for they did not understand the world situation: the worker of England corrupted by imperialist profits; the Commune defeated in Paris; the recent triumph of the bourgeois national movement in Germany; the age-long sleep of semi-feudal Russia. Marx and Engels gauged the times accurately; they understood the international situation; they realised that the approach to the beginning of the social revolution must be slow." (*Ibid.*, pp. 74-75.)

In *The State and Revolution*, Lenin wrote:

"The anarchists had tried to claim the Paris Commune as their 'own,' so to say, as a corroboration of their doctrine; and they betrayed utter inability to understand its lessons and Marx's analysis of these lessons. Anarchism has failed to give anything even approaching a true solution of the concrete political problems, *viz.*, must the old state machine be *smashed?* and *what* should supersede it?" (Chap. VI.)

For Bukharin's non-Marxist position on the question of the difference between Marxists and anarchists in their attitude to the state, see Lenin's article, "The Youth International," 1916 (*Collected Works*, Russian ed., Vol. XIX, pp. 295-96). On the question of the main theoretical difference between Marxism and anarchism, see also note 64.

99. In the text of the *Critique* in this edition all the passages omitted have been restored.

100. Kautsky was then editor of the *Neue Zeit*, the weekly theoretical organ of German Social-Democracy, in which Engels published Marx's *Critique*.

101. Of these papers the first two were Social-Democratic, the third bourgeois.

102. Engels is referring to the fact that when he sent Kautsky the text of Marx's *Critique of the Gotha Programme* for publication, he warned Kautsky that if it was not published in the *Neue Zeit* he (Engels) would publish it in the *Wiener Arbeiter-Zeitung*—i.e., that one way or another Marx's *Critique* would be made public.

103. W. Dietz (1843-1922); German Social-Democrat, member of the Reichstag, manager of the party publishing house in Stuttgart, which also issued the *Neue Zeit*. He always belonged to the Right opportunist wing of German Social-Democracy; during the World War he was a social-chauvinist.

104. Although in making his report at the Halle Congress in 1890 (see note 96), W. Liebknecht admitted that the old programme required revision, he nevertheless praised it in every possible way as the "battle standard," the "guiding star," of the party, etc. While analysing each point of the Gotha Programme separately, and in places putting forward the objections raised by Marx and Engels—but without mentioning their names—Liebknecht ended his examination of each point with the conclusion that the point was "indubitably" correct "in principle" or "in essence," even if it required re-editing. He attacked *only* the phrase about "the iron law of wages" and the demand for the establishment of producers' co-operative societies with state aid. On the question of the state, Liebknecht expressed the view that instead of the "free state," "it might be better to say: socialist society in the free state." In his concluding speech, Liebknecht dealt with the question of the transition period from capitalism to socialism as follows, without saying a

single word about the dictatorship of the proletariat: "The present-day state grows into the state of the future, just as the state of the fuure is already contained in the present-day state." (See *The Protocol of the Proceedings of the Halle Party Congress, October 12 to 18, 1890*, Berlin, 1890 [in German].)

105. For information about Bebel, see note 49; on his opposition to the publication of Marx's *Critique*, see note 92.

106. This reproach was directed above all against Kautsky. In his endeavours to weaken the effect produced in the leading circles of German Social-Democracy by Marx's criticism of Lassalleanism, Kautsky published in No. 21 of the *Neue Zeit* an article entitled "Our Programmes" in which he opportunistically diminished the practical significance of Marx's criticism, dissociated himself from it and emphasised the great "services" of Lassalle. Among other things, he said, "the standpoint which Marx adopted towards Lassalle is not the standpoint of German Social-Democracy.... Social-Democracy... has a different attitude to Lassalle from that of Marx.... How could we forget the man from whose writings all of us older party comrades and even the majority of the younger have derived their first socialist knowledge, their first enthusiasm for socialism! We study and examine attentively what Marx says about his pupil Lassalle, but we do not forget that the latter also was one of our first teachers and champions." (*Neue Zeit*, 1890-91, Vol. I, p. 680.) It was precisely this mistaken opportunist estimate of Lassalle that evoked Engels' sharp characterisation of Lassalle in this letter to Kautsky.

107. During nearly a decade (1845-54) Lassalle conducted, as a lawyer, the very complicated and for its time very sensational divorce case of the Countess Sophie Hatzfeld (1805-81), in the course of which he made use of the most varied lawyer's tricks.

108. During the period of the Anti-Socialist Law (1878-90) when all legal working class organisations were forbidden, the Social-Democratic fraction in the Reichstag was the highest organ of the party. Although the fraction consisted to a considerable extent of opportunists, the leadership of the party was in the hands of Bebel, who based himself on the masses of the party membership and on the illegal central organ, the *Sozialdemokrat*, published in Zurich and later in London. This paper was in general edited in accordance with the directions of Engels.

109. That is to say, the organisation of the Lassalleans, the General Association of German Workers, the leader of which from 1864 to 1871 was Johann Baptist Schweitzer (1833-75). Schweitzer was editor of the central organ, chairman of the party and a member of the Reichstag. He continued Lassalle's policy of intriguing with Bismarck who, as was revealed a few years ago, financed the paper. He guided the Association, following Lassalle's tradition, in a dictatorial fashion, attempting to maintain his dictatorial power even when a strong opposition had developed against him, and he endeavoured to extend

# EXPLANATORY NOTES

this power to the trade union organisations, the foundation of which—only under the pressure of the masses, it is true—he had begun in 1868.

110. The leading article in the *Vorwärts*, the central organ of German Social-Democracy, expressed the official position of the party leadership on Marx's *Critique*. The article contained a sharp condemnation of Marx's estimate of Lassalle and considered it a merit of the party that it had accepted the Gotha draft programme in opposition to Marx's opinion. It was further asserted in the article that the development of the party had proved Marx wrong, and that the Social-Democratic fraction in the Reichstag and the party leadership had in no case expressed their agreement to the publication of the *Critique*. The article also states: "The German Social-Democrats are not Marxians, not Lassalleans—they are Social-Democrats." (*Neue Zeit*, 1890-91, Vol. I, p. 684.)

111. Liebknecht intended to write a special article on the history of the Gotha Programme for the *Neue Zeit*, which, according to Kautsky, "would give a history of our party programme in general and particularly of those conditions which made it possible for the Gotha Programme in 1875 to represent the expression of the theoretical consciousness of the majority of the party." (*Ibid.*, p. 681.) Kautsky wrote in the above-mentioned article, entitled "Our Programmes": "In this respect ... the programme letter required a supplement. Engels could not give this."

112. The reference is to the fourth edition of Engels' book, *The Origin of the Family, Private Property and the State*, published by the Stuttgart publishing house (Verlay Dietz) of the party.

113. Richard Fischer (1855-1926); member of the Executive of the Social-Democratic Party; manager of the Berlin party publishing house.

114. In 1891 Engels wrote prefaces to the newly re-published works of Marx, *The Civil War in France* and *Wage-Labour and Capital* and to his own pamphlet, *Socialism: Utopian and Scientific*.

115. The draft programme, criticised by Marx and Engels in March-May, 1875, was adopted by the Unity Congress of the Eisenachers and Lassalleans at Gotha on May 25, 1875. The congress made some changes and additions to the text. With the exception of some of the additions to the concrete demands, all these changes are noted in footnotes. All those new formulations that express the influence of Marx's criticism, even if only to a slight degree, are shown in italics, together with a reference to the corresponding page of the *Critique*. The reader will observe that Marx's suggestions were taken notice of only to a very slight extent. The programme adopted by the congress was given the title: *Programme of the Socialist Workers' Party of Germany*, and in the text "German Workers' Party" was altered throughout to "Socialist Workers' Party of Germany."

116. The text of this point as finally adopted by the congress reads: "Labour is the source of all wealth and all culture, and inasmuch as generally useful

labour is possible only through society, the total product of labour belongs to society, *i.e.*, to all its members, with universal obligation to work, with equal right, to each according to his reasonable needs."

117. The final text reads: "The emancipation of labour demands the *conversion* of the instruments of labour into the common property of society and the co-operative regulation of the total labour, with employment for common use of the proceeds of labour and their equitable distribution." (See p. 6.)

118. The final text reads: "The Socialist Workers' Party of Germany, *although* acting in the first place within *national limits*, is conscious of the *international character of the workers' movement* and is resolved to fulfil all the *obligations* which this imposes on the workers in order to make the brotherhood of all men a truth." (See pp. 12-13, 19.)

119. The final text of the second part of this point reads: "... strives for ... the breaking of the iron law of wages by the abolition of the *system of wage-labour*, the abolition of exploitation in every form, the removal of all social and political inequality." (See pp. 14-15.)

120. Section A was joined with section B, and section C with section D. The introductory phrase of the first section, which contains six points, runs: "The Socialist Workers' Party of Germany demands as the foundations of the state." The expression used in the draft—*"as the free basis"*—was deleted. (See p. 17.)

121. This phrase was dropped in the final editing.

122. This point was deleted (see p. 21), but there was added to the next point, point 4: "Repeal of all exceptional laws, especially the press, association and assembly laws, and in general of all laws which restrict free expression of opinion, free investigation and thought"; the following addition was made to the sixth point: *"Declaration that religion is a private matter."*

123. In the final text the introduction of the second section, which contains eight points, runs: "The Socialist Workers' Party of Germany demands, within existing society."

124. In the final editing this sentence was deleted.

125. In the final text: "A normal working day, corresponding to the needs of society." (See p. 21.)

126. In the final text: "The prohibition of child labour and of all women's labour that is *harmful to health and morals*." (See p. 22.)

127. The final text reads: "Legislation protecting the lives and health of the workers. Sanitary control of workers' quarters. Supervision of mines, factory, workshop and home industries by officials *elected by the workers*." (See p. 22.)